Night Games

Bartending At Max McGee's and Fuzzy Thurston's Left Guard and other bistros

by Bob Dries

DEDICATION

Dedicated to the Green Bay Packers, then, now and foever.
And to all the lovely, lovely women.

CONTENTS

ACKNOWLEDGMENTS

This book exists because of my good friend Paul Bentzen. During the years of 1965 to 1972 I either frequently drank or worked behind the bar at The Left Guard in Appleton, Wisconsin. The Guard, as it was know locally, was owned and operated by Max McGee and Fuzzy Thurston, the left end and the left guard, respectively, of the Lombardi-era Green Bay Packers. With that pedigree, it quickly became the favorite spot for Packer players on their Monday nights off. And, of course, also on those evenings when they celebrated some of the Packer's classic victories of that wonderful era.

One night, after regaling Paul--also a life-long Packer fan-- at our local watering hole in Spring Green, Wisconsin, with a number of stories about my experiences there, he said:

"You should write these down. It would make a great book."

Paul is a professional actor and has performed in countless plays in various roles during his 30 year career at American Players Theater and other theaters throughout the country. So I took his comment as highly credible. However, a great book requires a great writer. Ladies and gentlemen, I am not a great writer. However, I am hoping that I am a good enough writer to have created a book you will enjoy. You, of course, will have to decide.

Once I began to write, I soon realized that, although my years working at The Left Guard had given me a lot of wonderful memories of good times, other people and other places had done the same. So I have included those stories as well.

Since this is a book about real events it was necessary to name real people. Many names of the people I write about will be familiar to anyone who has followed professional football. However, just as a really good play or movie requires a fine supporting cast, so too does this book. So, in addition to the famous, many of the others named are those who, although not famous, did contribute to the rich fabric of these stories.

And thus, my closing point. In all the countless hours I stood behind the bar and served Max, Fuzzy and the rest of the Packer players, never once was any one of them ever arrogant, abusive or unkind. Regardless of the lateness of the hour, the amount of liquor consumed, the mouthing off of a drunken customer, they were always unfailingly courteous, respectful and generous to anyone around them, but especially to those of us working there. This was also true of any of the NFL players from other teams of that era who stepped into the Left Guard. And so, it would bother me a great deal if I would write anything harmful or hurtful about any of them. Or anyone else in this book. So, regarding identities, in some instances I have either omitted last names or changed them entirely when it seemed prudent.

And after all these years I'd also like to say a big thank you to those Packer greats, Fuzzy Thruston and Max McGee. Fuzzy, I hope you enjoy this book. And Max, it broke my heart when I heard of your demise. I only wish I'd written this sooner as I think you'd have enjoyed it as well.

Bob Dries

Spring Green, Wisconsin

Winter, 2012

1
MY DAY IN COURT

My career in the food and beverage industry began because I was serving a two year term of probation for contributing to the delinquency of a minor child. This minor child, a girl of seventeen who acted, dressed and screwed like a twenty five-year old hooker, thought she was pregnant. When she confided in her divorced father, he became upset and went to the police, demanding satisfaction. The police, after interrogating the victim, went back and, as tactfully as possible given the circumstances, told the father that his daughter had indicated there might be more than one perpetrator doing the penetrating. How many? Well, sir, five actually. But not all at once, you understand

Five? OK, now he was really angry. Confronted with having to choose between the fact that he had raised a daughter who at the age of seventeen was banging any and all of the teen age hoodlums that hung around downtown West Allis or that she had been a poor, misguided lamb wantonly led to the slaughter, he did what any self-respecting father would do. He chose the lamb.

As a result late one April morning, Ronny, Dave and myself stood before Judge Christ T. Seraphim in a Milwaukee courtroom. Since we three were all 18 or older, we were the big time criminals. Jason and Kenny, being minors, were not present. They would be dealt with in a juvenile court.

Judge Seraphim held a popular court. This was before TV was ever allowed in courtrooms, and his was always packed with spectators, law students and other lawyers who had time to waste between cases. The newspaper reporters and other media types loved being assigned there, since the Judge went out of his way to make his cases interesting. An extremely strict mendicant, he'd already made headlines several times because of his courtroom antics of openly mocking or goading defendants, handing down unusual punishments and the like. The opinion on the street was he was a self-righteous prick who liked to lock people up. Later in his career he would resign in disgrace after groping a woman as they rode in an elevator together, a story I recall reading several times over with a great deal of pleasure.

That morning as we entered the courtroom and waited for our case to be called, he looked over at us with a salivating smile. In a few minutes I found out why. Evidently we were destined to the highlight of his morning. Already uneasy, my stomach lurched. Although I had known I was in trouble I began to realize at that moment that it could be far more serious than I anticipated.

At eighteen, I was the youngest of our three wrong-doers and aside from minor run-ins with the cops for the stupid things you do as a teen-ager, I had no real criminal past. I had no criminal record, no experience with being treated as an adult by the courts and police. Ronny however, at nineteen, was already on probation for burglary. Dave, twenty three years old, was deathly pale and had not spoken a word to either of us since we'd been locked up in the bull pen earlier. He knew that, at his age, he would likely receive the harshest treatment by the judge. He also had a police record for theft and assault.

In spite of their criminal pasts, I had never seen either one of my co-defendants do anything seriously criminal in the year or so I had known them. Mostly we, and a lot of others our age, hung together in a loose confederation of punks in the all-night restaurants in downtown West Allis or on the street corners of Greenfield Avenue. Edgy as tomcats, we waited for any opportunity that arose to party at someone's house or apartment, and, lacking that, go cruising in cars, go to dances, try and sometimes succeed in buying booze and beer with fake i.d.'s, try and sometimes succeed in getting laid where ever and whenever we could --all those things that still go on today in those peculiar no-man land years of 18 to 21. I think the most serious thing I'd done up to then was siphon gas one night from a truck for a buddy's car when we were too broke to buy it. So, up until that moment when Seraphim gave off that wolfish smile, I guess I was the epitome of the person who wasn't worried because he didn't know how serious things really were.

My attitude was also based on my interactions regarding my case. I was living at home with my parents and my sister when one evening the phone rang. It was Detective Meyers with the West Allis Police.

Bob, we have something we need to talk over. Could you stop by the station?

What about?"

A Janet _____ . I think we can get it straightened out about a half an hour.

So a couple of nights later I'm sitting across the desk from Meyers, an overweight guy with glasses and an easy-going avuncular manner. Now, in defense of what is going to appear to be an incredibly large amount of stupidity on my part, these were the good old days before Miranda. None of this "you have the right" crap. Just a good old talk man-to-man, about how this little hussy got all hot and of course you did what any red-blooded American Pie boy would do and gave her a shot in the panties. It was only when he paused and reached below the desk and I heard the click of a tape recorder being shut off that I began to feel that maybe I'd been had.

"Well, her father is damn upset," Meyers said coldly, his mood changing abruptly as he got up and ushered me out of his office. "So you're going to have to go to court. But you won't be alone. It won't amount to much. I'll let you know the court date. In the meantime don't do anything stupid to make it worse."

I didn't do anything to make it worse. I didn't have to. It reached the pinnacle of disaster all on its own that morning when I went to trial and the victim was called in the courtroom to testify. The only other times I'd seen her prior to then she wore bright red lipstick, Bette Davis eyes dripping with mascara, tight sweaters with no bra underneath and fatigue pants that outlined a sweet bootie which wiggled in invitation when ever she walked. Or else she was totally bare-assed. Now however, with no make-up, face pale, eyes red and swollen from evident tears of remorse, she approached the witness chair clad in a loose fitting Mother Hubbard-type dress, head bowed in obvious shame. She looked about twelve years old. A sympathetic murmur rose for the gallery.

"Shit," Ronny muttered. "We're screwed."

We had a public defender. The charges were read and after identifying himself as our counsel, this clown-boy remained silent for the entire trial, evidently well aware he shouldn't interfere with the judge's fun. So Seraphim, with an open field of fire, began to shoot his ducks.

"You've had intercourse with these three buys?" he asked her incredulously.

Yes, she answered, her voice barely audible.

"All three at once?" Salacious titter from the gallery.

No, your honor. Separately. All except Dave.

"Dave? Which one is Dave? Why not?"

"We were going to and then he stopped."

This of course was total bullshit. Dave had banged her more than any of us. But I think she realized that with his being over twenty one and with his record, he'd probably get sent to prison. And I realized that, in spite of the bitterness I felt towards her, this whole thing was probably not what she wanted either. Thinking herself pregnant, she'd panicked, ran to daddy, and from then on it had snowballed into a potential disaster for all of us.

"Stopped? Then why is he being charged?" he asked the assistant D.A.

"According to the police statement, she stated that she had had intercourse with all three of these defendants, Your Honor. We can drop the charges against Mr. Christy if she testifies otherwise."

"I don't think so," the judge replied. He looked over to the witness. "So he stopped. Did he have his pants down?"

Again the gallery tittered. Oh boy. Here we go.

Yes.

"Yes? Well then, honey, did you see his privates?"

Open chuckles behind us now.

She sensed a trap. No.

"No? Why not?"

I had my eyes closed.

"Too bad. We could charge him with lewd and lascivious behavior in front of a minor child."

He turned his gaze back to us.

"But these other guys, they did have intercourse with you?"

Yes, Your Honor.

"Did you have your eyes open with them?"

She shook her head.

Seraphim turned to the assistant DA again. "Well, maybe we should add the lewd and lascivious charge to them anyway?"

The rotten bastard. He was playing with us.

"You guys got jobs?" he asked, directly his attention back to us. " Did you graduate from high school?"

Ronny and Dave shook their heads.

"Yes, Your Honor," I replied.

"Where from?"

"Marquette University High School." His eyebrows

rose in surprise. Marquette was a tony college-prep school and I'm quite sure until then he'd never had a MUHS grad standing in front of him. "I'm working at a Shell station until fall when I'll start college," I added.

The last part was a lie but I figured it was worth a shot. I don't know if it made a difference or not but the judge, glancing at the clock and at the line up of cases still waiting in the courtroom, decided he'd had enough fun.

"Sheppay and Christy, each a year in Milwaukee County jail. Dries, two years probation."

Bang went the gavel.

2
IT'S GREEK TO ME

Three days later I reported to my probation officer. But before that I had to go home and break the news. I had not mentioned a word about my dilemma to my parents, hoping desperately that somehow it would somehow magically vanish. It was not pleasant.

"My God!" my mother exclaimed. "What if it's in the papers?"

My sister was due to be married in a few months and her wedding announcement had already been published in the Milwaukee Journal. This, admittedly, would not be a good follow-up. My father alternated between bouts of expressing his anger in my actions, disappointment in my lack of appreciation for all they'd done for me and amazement at the depths of my stupidity. I sat silently at the kitchen table, head bowed, knowing I deserved every bit of their wrath.

My patents, staunch blue-collar Catholics, had raised my older brother and two older sisters with very little problem. My brother had worked his way through both high school and college and had gotten a degree in engineering, the first in our family to do so. Both of my sisters had done well in school. The youngest had received scholarships for both high school and college while the older one had also excelled and, after working for several years in an executive office, was currently married and raising a family. And then there was me.

I hated school. From first grade on, I found it boring, restrictive and irrelevant. I had learned to read by the time I was five. We did not have a television in our house and either my mother or father would read to me almost every evening at a very early age. I was particularly fond of stories from the Bible history. However, after working all day, sometimes they were too tired or had additional work to do. My mother, who had taught school prior to her marriage, solved this problem by eliminating the middleman. She taught me how to read.

Also at this time schools were quite different, especially Catholic schools. Generally class size numbered well over 40 pupils, taught by nuns. Lumped together like cattle, we were all treated the same. There were no special classes, no recognition that some of us may be ahead or behind of others. The nuns believed they were called to join a religious order by God. Well, if that's the case, I wish he had done a hell of a lot better job in calling a few of them that could actually teach.

By the time I left third grade I was labeled as "a bad actor." By fifth grade the nuns had personally taken upon themselves the mission of ridding me of the devil, which usually meant slapping me on my head and face or beating me with their fists up and down my back when I smarted off. Which, I readily admit, was often. I did not like them. So I would dream up ways to anger them, goad them into losing their temper. I put up with it, because this was an era where the adult attitude was generally that if any authority figure was slapping you around, you probably deserved it.

Aside from a few of my fellow devil-possessed pupils, because of my behavior the rest of the class avoided me. But that was ok with me. Most of them lived close to the school, in an up-scale area of pricey homes, parkways and classy shops, with fathers who were owners of successful companies, or lawyers, doctors and the like. I, with my blue collar background, lived in a working class neighborhood. Although our house was very nice, on a lovely street lined with elms, to reach it you would pass by an area of machine shops and cement factories. The closest store, a block from our house, looked like something you'd find in Dogpatch. I became a loner in class and, much to my parents dismay, began to hang around in the evenings with the hoodlum types living in my own neighborhood. These blue-collar sons and daughters, with similar working-class values and backgrounds, accepted me. I learned to smoke, curse, spit and began to wear my hair in an owl. I became adept at shop-lifting and feeling up girls.

Although I applied to and was accepted to Marquette University High School after grade school, it did not change my behavior since Marquette was virtually identical as my grade school socially. I continued to live in two very different worlds until I graduated. Then I went completely over to my hoodlum pals.

My probation officer was a middle-aged man who bore the weary look of someone who spends a lot of time dealing with the bad elements of society. Compared to most of his cases, mine must have seemed to him fairly petty. The first visit lasted no longer than fifteen minutes.

"Get a job,"he told me. "Stay away from your hoodlum friends. If you get in trouble again, you'll go to jail."

He also said I should call him once a week, or more if I needed to, and he would tell me when to report in person. He would also work on getting my charge reduced, since contributing to the delinquency of a minor was a felony. He might get it reduced to fornication, a misdemeanor.

"But that won't be possible if you get in trouble again,' he warned.

At home I scanned the help-wanted ads.

Porter wanted. Apply in person, 8 am to 4 pm Mon thru Fri. Sands Motel.

1800 W. Bluemond Rd.

The Sands was a classy motel owned and operated by two Greek brothers named C. It was a new 80 unit building built around a courtyard, with a modern brick exterior. Located on busy Bluemond Road in Wauwatosa, it was already doing a good business. The brothers also owned a commercial laundry. The laundry, a family business, had been started by their mother who had come to this country from Greece. After their father died, she began to take in laundry from the neighbors to support her family and, being a shrewd lady, built the business into a major venture. The sons, looking to increase the family holdings, chose to build the Sands. It made sense, since one of the major expenses for a motel is its laundry bill. So, not only was a profit made on the room rentals, but also on sending the dirty linens to their own laundry for washing as well.

In addition to the rooms, a coffee shop, cocktail lounge, formal dining room and banquet room also provided revenue. A good-sized indoor pool was also on the premises. I got the job and quickly learned that a porter was pretty much a glorified janitor. I mostly worked days, and my duties were varied and for the most part interesting. I cleaned and maintained the pool, mowed grass in the summer and plowed snow in the winter, changed the lettering daily to show the dining room specials on a large marquee sign next to Bluemound Rd, did minor mechanical repairs on various pieces of equipment, repaired broken drapery and plumbing in the rooms, and delivered room service.

One morning I carried a tray with two breakfasts to a room. After I knocked on the door, a voice bade me enter. When I did, I discovered my buddy's mother tucked under the covers. The man who stood by the door, clad in his pants and undershirt, was definitely not her husband. I discreetly kept my eyes down and set the tray on the dressing table, while she burrowed under the covers. The man signed the bill and rummaged in his pockets for some change.

"Geez, Fred, give the kid some bills," came the voice from under the covers.

Fred shot her a look and then pulled some singles out of his wallet. I took my hush money, thanked him, and left.

The brothers, whom I shall call Phil and Costas, were quite a pair. Costas, the younger, ran the entire motel operation. He was a good looking guy, dressed sharp, and had a very pretty wife and a couple of young kids. He smoked thin cigars and was very good at dealing with people. To my knowledge he never messed around on his wife. We got along well, primarily I think because I did my job to his satisfaction. He knew quite a bit about all the equipment needed to keep the entire operation functioning and he often would show me how to fix and maintain the cooling units, plumbing, pool equipment, stoves and ovens and the rest.

Phil was bulkier in build, rather plain faced, dressed in a suit, and wore dark-rimmed glasses. He was much more confrontational, and most of the help tried to avoid him. Although in theory his job was to run the laundry, he'd often stop into the motel and meddle in its affairs, irritating Costas a good deal. He was also married but was having an affair with a red-headed waitress who worked in the coffee shop.

Although the brothers hired dishwashers for the coffee shop, often they would not show up. I'd get the call to go over and wash dishes. Since the cook would wait til mid-morning before giving up on the no-show, by the time I arrived after a busy morning the kitchen floor would be covered with heaping bus pans of dirty dishes. It was a very discouraging sight but fortunately the cook, Paul, helped me out. Paul was Greek, and prior to cooking, he had worked as a dishwasher, busboy, and bellhop in New York, and had great stories about these experiences. He taught me two things, the first how to say shit in Greek--skata--, the second a system of scraping and sorting dirty dishes that was incredibly fast. But after I ran the last rack of dishes through that first morning he pulled me aside.

"Bob, I'll tell Costas that I helped you. Otherwise, if they find out you did all these dishes this quick, they won't hire another dishwasher. You'll get stuck doing them all the time. If they send you over here again, go slower."

I took his advice and the next time, I slowed down.

One of the busboys they hired for the coffee shop was a white-bread looking high school kid who, although he could not speak Greek, had grown up in a home where his parents spoke it, so he could understand it. One of the C. brothers favorite tricks was to speak in Greek to each other in front of the help when they wanted to talk about something they didn't want us to hear. Paul of course could understand them but they would wait until he was out of earshot. Now however, with Ernie in out midst, we had a spy, since they were not aware he could understand Greek.

"Phil was bitching to Costas that the coffee shop till was short the other day," he would report to us after one such conversation. "Costas wanted to know how he knew but Phil wouldn't say. Costas asked him if Audrey told him. That pissed Phil off." We grinned, since Audrey was Phil's mistress. "Then Costas told him that he ought to keep his dick in his pants or it would cost him a lot of money sometime."

But after while Ernie got tired of us pestering him whenever the brothers would do their routine. So he began to feed us false information.

"Hey Bob," he took me aside one day. "Phil told Costas he should fire you cause he heard you say you wanted to bang his wife."

Damn, I thought, nervously searching my memory for my blunder, knowing full well it was quite possible I did say such a thing. For a week I furtively watched Costas whenever we passed, looking for some sign of impending doom.

On other occasions he would tell the various waitresses that Chris or Phil had made lewd or vulgar remarks about parts of their anatomy. One of the better waitresses got so mad when she heard that Phil said she had an ass "bigger than a Cadillac" that she quit in a huff, telling Phil during her exit that "he ought to take a look at his own fat Greek ass." Phil of course was baffled at the whole incident but sensed something was amiss. Also, her quitting angered the other women and Ernie realized he may have gone too far. However, he maintained his innocence, claiming that what he'd related was true. Anyway, after that he pretty much refused to offer any more translations so we lost our secret agent.

The brothers were often very competitive between themselves. One day after an especially busy week-end Costas had me take a big load of dirty bedding over to the laundry. When I arrived I jumped down from the van, went inside and asked where I should unload it. The shop manager went into Phil's office and a moment later Phil came out.

"Bob, what the hell you doing with that laundry?" he snapped.

"Costas told me to bring it here.

"Well, he doesn't run the laundry. We're already got more than we can handle today. Take it back."

Back I went. I barely pulled up when Costas came over and looked inside.

"Bob, I thought I told you to take that bedding to the laundry."

"I did. Phil said they were too busy and to bring it back."

"Well, goddamn, I can' t run a motel without clean bedding. Take it over there. I'll call him."

I drove back to the laundry. This time Phil didn't come out of his office when he heard of my arrival. After sitting there about thirty minutes, the shop manager came out.

"Phil said to take it back to the motel and to tell Costas he should plan better than this."

Once more I drove back. Costas's face flushed in anger when I delivered the message.

"Screw him. Goddammit, you drive back there and dump it on the loading dock if you have to."

I did as I was told. Just about the time I got it all piled on the loading dock, Phil came out, mad as hell, and chewed me out. He finished with words to the effect that "if you value your goddamn job you get those sheets back in the van and tell Chris to stick them up his ass."

As I drove off the shop manager was looking out the laundry window, grinning as he gave me a thumbs up. I started grinning too. The whole thing was pretty funny. By now the morning had passed and if these guys wanted to have a war over bedsheets it was all right with me. And war they did. I spent the rest of my day driving the van back and forth and delivering messages that got nastier right along. It was pretty easy work. At quitting time I locked up the van, still loaded with dirty sheets, in the motel lot and went home. When I returned the next morning the van was empty. I never found out how the sheet war ended.

Overall it was a pretty good job. I continued to work there for the next two years, and, although my parents were disappointed that I showed no interest in going on to college, at least I was working. I got a couple of raises, I had my own car, a sweet, beautiful girl friend, and I finished my probation. True to his word, my P.O. had gotten my charge reduced to fornication.

A couple of things happened before I left my employment there which moved my career forward. One Saturday night a large wedding had been booked. Earlier in the week I overheard George, the bar manager, telling Costas he needed to find a bartender to serve the drinks at the portable bar which would be set up in the banquet room.

"I can do that," I volunteered. Costas and George exchanged looks and I could see they liked the idea. It would save them the hassle of finding someone, they could trust me not to steal very much, and my wage would be at my regular rate, not nearly as much as would be paid to a experienced bartender. The last item especially appealed to Costas. On the downside, I had zero experience, and was not yet twenty one. George said he felt the age issue not significant since he would be working in the same room, at another bar. And the odds of anyone checking on my age were virtually non-existent. As for experience, the mixed drinks would be limited to Manhattans, martinis and highballs, and pouring the beer from the keg paid for by the groom.

I showed up an hour before the reception started in a white shirt and black slacks, and put on an ornate gold braided bartender's vest that made me look like I knew what I was doing. After a fifteen minute crash course in mixing drinks, the reception started. We got slammed, busy as hell. I performed adequately, made some money in tips, and even managed to flirt with some of the drunken ladies. I drove home thinking I liked being a bartender a lot, especially compared to my regular duties. From then on I began to work tending bar at weddings and private parties whenever possible.

About the same time, Costas hired a new food manager. Although he ran the entire operation, each part—motel, food and banquets, bar—had its own manager.

The new manager was an Italian guy named Frank Guillatti, who had a big nose and, while working as host to seat customers in the dining room, would slap the menus against his leg. After a couple of months Frank moved on. Before he left he took me aside.

"Bob, I'm going to work at a Nino's Steak Round-up opening up on Howell Avenue. Come and see me in a couple of days. We're looking for good people."

No one had ever said I was good at anything in a long time. Two weeks later I began work at Nino's.

3

MOVING ON UP TO NINO'S

The original Nino's Steak Round Up was a successful downtown Milwaukee restaurant specializing in charcoal broiled steaks. Where most other up-scale restaurants served steaks as part of a large varied menu, at Nino's they made up 95% of the menu. Another feature was that they were actually charcoal broiled on a grill located in the dining room, visible to the customers, rather than on a gas broiler in the kitchen like virtually all other restaurants did at the time. The menu at Nino's featured a large steak selection, and all entrees were served with a large lettuce only salad, baked potato and rolls and butter. Period. No frills, just good red meat charcoal-broiled, at a good price. We were still in the era where the fact that carbonized, burnt animal flesh could give you cancer was unknown, and business was great.

The chefs were all Negroes, men who took great pride in their appearance and even greater pride in their considerable ability to broil meat to perfection. It was not an easy job. The grill was at about waist height, twelve feet in length, and about three feet in depth. On a busy Saturday night, at any given time it would be virtually covered with various cuts of steak, at varying stages of doneness. Dressed in white coats and those big, mushroom- shaped hats, the chefs would spin and pirouette as they pulled off the appropriate cuts of meat for each order with silver tongs and place them on one of the serving braziers heated with live coals that were lined up atop the stainless steel serving counter. After adding the correct number of baked potatoes from warmers below the grill, they grabbed a hand-held mike and would call out the waitress's number in a stylized voice intelligible only to the waitresses and other employees. The waitress would then show up with a serving cart where she loaded plates from a plate warmer near by, then the brazier with its sizzling steaks and potatoes, and proceed to the customers table. The impact of those steaks arriving at table side, hissing and piping hot in their fragrant juices, filling the air with their wonderful aroma, never failed to elicit oohs and aahs of anticipation and cause mouths to start to water.

Nino Costarella owned and operated the business. After a string of owning restaurants that failed, he used this experience to devise the concept currently at Nino's that brought him so much success . He never advertised, refusing all sales attempts by saying "The year I went broke I spent $5,000 on advertising. If you put the money in the product, it'll advertise itself." He developed a unique, defined decor of interior walls covered in rustic stone, western paintings and enormous steer horns. The logo on napkins, menus and signs was a modern, stylized rendition of a steer head. He worked hard, practiced a hands-on style of management, and made sure the quality of the food and drinks was always both good and consistent. Now, after ten years of success at the downtown location, he had begun to expand. The second location, on Highway 100 and Capital Drive, managed by his son Louie, was about three years old. Although smaller than the downtown location, it also did a thriving business. The Howell Avenue operation was to be the third Nino's to open in Milwaukee.

One Christmas, after I had worked my way up to a management position, Nino gave me the gift of a tie tack of the Nino's logo, in silver and gold, with diamonds as the steer's eyes. After I left the organization I rarely wore a tie so I took mine to a jeweler who crafted it into a ring which I still have and treasure, both for its uniqueness and the good memories it inspires.

A prime example of Nino's business acumen was the way he picked locations for his new restaurants. He was partial to sites where, in spite of bustling surroundings, other business had not been able to survive. Owners of these location were generally anxious to either sell or lease the property and Nino could get favorable terms. He would then gut the structure, call in his horde of craftsman and transform the interior with his decor. The Howell Avenue location was one such location. Directly across from Mitchell Field, Milwaukee's airport, the only other supper club close by was a Japanese place about five miles away. This Nino's was the largest in floor area so far, occupying the entire first floor with a two story motel above, and held a large barroom, two dining rooms and a banquet hall. Around it there was plenty of parking.

As Nino began his preparations to open the Howell Avenue location, he got a call from a friend of his who worked at the Sheboygan County Sheriff's Department.

"Nino, we got a guy here in jail. He's an artist that paints western pictures. He doesn't have enough money to pay his fine and he's looking to sell some of his paintings. I think you might be interested."

Nino was indeed interested. Up to this point all the pictures of western scenes hanging on the walls of in his restaurants were prints, reproductions of paintings by Remington, Russell and other well-known artists of the Old West. He drove to Sheboygan where he was introduced to Charles Damrow who was serving a brief jail sentence for a disorderly conduct charge since he was unable to pay his fine. Nino agreed to pay his fine in return for two paintings. By the time the deal was worked out and Charlie released, the two men had discovered they were kindred spirits.

Charlie got in his van and followed Nino to Milwaukee. Charlie's van was a reflection of his personality. This was a couple of years before the Hippie-style VW live-in vans became prevalent, and Charlie was a forerunner. He had bought a step-van of the type typically used for making commercial bakery deliveries. He had painted it a two-tone brown and green accented by numerous North American Indian symbols to honor his Ojibwa heritage. Inside he had a bunk, a small sink and hot plate and a television. The antenna for the TV was attached on one of the exterior back doors, and rose above the roof. It was very unique at the time, and always caused a stir when it went down the street.

Upon his arrival Nino got Charlie established in an apartment where he became Nino's painter-in-residence. He would come into the bar in the afternoon and drink slowly and quietly. After an early dinner he would go back to his apartment and paint. Once a month his tab for food and drink would be tallied and then applied to the cost of one of his paintings. In time he met a waitress at the downtown location by the name of Nori and they became lovers. I met Charlie, when, as we were working on the final touches at Howell Avenue, Nino picked up the phone and called him.

"Charlie, come here and take a look at this bar. I want a picture that'll stand out on one of the walls."

Charlie arrived and he and Nino talked things over. The wall in question was a lengthy unbroken expanse recently covered with Nino's trademark decorative stone. The walls adjacent were shorter, one of them containing windows, while the other was the backdrop to the piano bar. The fourth wall was behind the u-shaped bar. These walls would hold smaller paintings. But for the big wall, Nino wanted something large and dramatic. After a while

Charlie left. Two days later he called. He was on his way, the painting carefully wrapped and strapped to the side of his van. When he arrived we helped him carry it in, and leaned it against the wall where it was unwrapped.

"Careful," Charlie admonished. "The paint may still be damp."

It was large, about six by eight feet. And it was magnificent. Two huge, dark bull buffaloes reared up on their back hooves, shaggy heads lowered, battling in the moonlight. Behind them the rugged western landscape lay in brooding, mysterious night time splendor. It was absolutely perfect, for both the room and the wall on which it would be hung. Charlie had painted it non-stop over the last two days and nights. When it was hung in place, an accent light mounted above it provided the perfect illumination.

The Nino's chain has been long gone, a victim of changing tastes and dire health warnings about burnt animal flesh. At its height it consisted of over a dozen restaurants in Wisconsin and adjacent states. Nino himself died while still in his fifties, this strong-willed, intelligent, dynamic man unable to overcome his addiction to Camel cigarettes. Despite warnings from his doctor and having a father who died of lung cancer, he continued to smoke, even after being diagnosed with throat cancer. And by now Charlie and Nori are probably gone as well. But occasionally when I think about the magnificence of that painting, I hope that it has survived, that somewhere it is hanging on a wall, and those two buffaloes are still battling in the moonlight. And someone still looks at in in admiration and awe as we did that day it was unwrapped, and many nights thereafter.

My work at Nino's was similar to my job at the Sands. I cleaned the charcoal grill daily, scraping and wire-brushing the grates, removing and washing the steel filters located in the big exhaust hood above by sending them well-soaped through the dishwasher. This was extremely important, because the daily broiling of the steaks caused a large amount of grease to solidify from the smoke as it was drawn up and out the vent system. In spite of having an automatic chemical fire suppression system above the broiler, a spark traveling upward could start a grease fire in the hood, and travel up the duct work, causing considerable damage in a short time due to its speed and intensity. Chaos resulted when this happened. The fire system would go off, dumping a huge amount of white chemical fire suppressant all over the steaks and broiler area, ruining the meat and shutting down operations until the mess was cleaned up. The fire extinguishing system would have to be recharged and made operational again before we could re-open. Smoke would fill the entire dining room, requiring the setting up of numerous big fans to air it out. An automatic alarm signal would be sent to the fire department and firemen, complete with pointy hats, clad in rubber coats and boots, would swarm into the place, axes in hand, determined to chop holes in the walls to determine the extent of the fire. They dragged in long hoses like fat snakes through the doors behind them, leaking at the joints and sopping the carpet. By the time they left it would take a couple of days to clean up.

I would also mop behind the bar, empty the trash containers, and stock its beer coolers and ice bins. Other duties included setting up tables and chairs for banquets and helping out the chefs and other kitchen help where needed.

Nino had no interest in the motel operation and it was its own separate business. However, a stipulation in his lease required him to provide breakfast hours in the dining room for motel guests. Serving began at 7 am until 11 am when lunch started. The business never amounted to much, so generally it was handled by one waitress and a breakfast cook.

One morning after I'd been there close to a year, the cook didn't show up. When I arrived at my usual start time of 7 am the waitress was in a minor panic. A call had been placed to one of the broiler chefs who could fill in but he lived a goodly ways away, and would not be there for some time. I seized the opportunity.

"Heck, I can cook breakfast. I did it on my other job." This was not strictly true. Once or twice I'd watched over a couple of eggs sizzling on the grill at the Sands Coffee shop when Paul had to go to the bathroom. But I was eager to make more money and tired of doing only grunt work.

Since there were few customers that morning I

managed to get by ok. The waitress gave a favorable report to Ann N., who was the manager and also owned part of the operation. Prior to her running the place, for many years she had been Nino's secretary. Before that she'd worked as a dancer at a night club he owned. The size of the diamond on her finger that Nino had given her one Christmas showed that theirs was a special relationship indeed.

I got promoted to breakfast cook and salad prep with a raise in pay. My first couple of weeks were rough. Although I was teaching myself, and--may I say in all modesty--a quick learner, there were still a number of breakfasts that got tossed into the garbage, both before and after they left the kitchen. I got pretty good at scrambled eggs, eggs over easy, medium or hard, but to this day I still don't know what the hell a three minute egg is supposed to be. Fortunately the orders for them were rare, which was good since I hated to make them. And at first my pancakes resembled hockey pucks but soon they too improved.

After the breakfast orders slowed I would begin to prepare salads, dressings and start the baked potatoes for the lunch and dinner clientele. One time I'd just finished my breakfast duties when Mary, the waitress, came back into the kitchen.

"I just waited on the sweetest girl. She said she was a singer. But I never heard of her. She left me an autographed copy of her record." A 45 in a paper cover dangled from her finger. I grabbed it and had a heart attack.

It was "Different Drum," by Linda Ronstadt and the Stone Poneys.

"Is she still here?" I yelled, running for the dining room. But sadly, it was vacant. She'd already left. "What did she order?" I demanded.

"Pancakes."

For a long time, when the opportunity was right, I'd casually mention to those around me that I'd made pancakes for Linda Ronstadt. Saying it truthfully, it had a ring of authenticity. It also suggested an intimacy in the listener's mind that I never felt necessary to correct.

After more months I again decided it was time to move up. I pressed Ann for a shot at bartending, elaborating my Sands experience a bit. She agreed. I would begin working banquets, and then gradually pick up hours at the main bar. But before I could begin, I had to get a bartenders license. I worriedly confessed to Ann about my criminal past. In my favor was the fact that I had completed my probation without incident and that my probation officer, God bless him, had indeed gone ahead and gotten the charge reduced to a misdemeanor. She said she'd talk to Nino.

The next time Nino visited we sat down at a table where I briefly told him what had happened.

"Go ahead and apply," he told me when I finished. "I know someone on the alcohol review board."

At this time to get a bartender's license in Milwaukee

you filled out an application, paid a fee, and got a blood test and a short-arm inspection at the city health department. The city would also run a check on you for a criminal background and then decide whether or not to issue the license. For those of you unfamiliar with the term, a short arm inspection is a euphemism for a physical inspection of your penis by a qualified medical person for signs of venereal disease. When I tell young people tending bar nowadays that I had to wave my pee-pee in front of a doc to get my bartenders license, they are positive I'm lying.

During the years I worked for Nino, I would discover on various occasions that he knew a number of people who could assist him when necessary. It was rumored that after his last bankruptcy he could no longer get a loan at a bank. So he had borrowed the money from the Mafia. There was indeed a Mafia presence in Milwaukee at this time, although not as notorious as in Chicago and other larger cities. A few years prior, Izzie Pogrob, the owner of a strip club in downtown Milwaukee called the Brass Rail was found shot gangland style in his pink Cadillac. His killer was never found, and the rumor was that the Mafia wanted his place and had made him an offer he unwisely refused. Other night clubs such as Gallagher's, The Holiday House, The Attic, The Scene and some others were rumored to be already owned and operated by Frank Balistrieri, the alleged Mafia don of Milwaukee.

With his Italian name and ancestry it was a given that some people might associate Nino with the mob. However, he never confirmed nor denied the financing rumor, nor did he ever volunteer where he did get the money to begin again. But then, as Ann put it once when some of us were discussing it, it was really no one's business.

A couple of years later, when I was promoted to day manager for the new store in Appleton, I was working with Nino, Ann, Louie, and John S. as we did the million things necessary in the last few days before we opened up the new operation. As we were working, a local building inspector came in and, openly hostile, wrote up a list of violations that needed to be corrected before we could open. The major problem was a hot water heater located in the wrong place. But moving it would take a couple of days. Nino politely protested, saying he had scheduled the opening for that week-end and asked could he go ahead and open and then get the problem corrected as soon as possible.

No way, the local inspector declared adamantly and stormed out of the building.

Nino stepped over to the phone, got a number out of his wallet, and dialed.

"Hello. This is Nino Costarella. Could I speak to the governor please?"

There was a response and then Nino hung up the phone and stood by, waiting. A few minutes later the phone rang.

"Hello Governor. Thank you for calling back. Yes, I'm

fine. And you?" A pause.

"Well, I'm opening up my new place in Appleton and I have a problem....."

The next day a state building inspector stopped by and checked over the list of violations. When he was finished he said, "You can open up this week-end. Get these items fixed as soon as possible, though. I'll go and talk to Mr._____ before I leave."

We had a successful opening. The following week the plumber moved the water heater, and when the local inspector came back he approved the job, and then apologized to Nino for his rude behavior. Nino graciously accepted and invited him in for a free dinner some time.

I passed all the hurdles, including my short arm exam, and got my license. Then, under the watchful tutelage of some very good professional bartenders, I began to learn the art of bartending. At this time bartending was considered a profession, a complex amalgam of physical stamina, manual dexterity, an excellent memory and math skills, a good personality and the ability to work under pressure without losing patience. You wore a white shirt, black slacks, a dark tie, and were neat, clean and left any personal problems behind when you stepped behind the bar. Drinks were mixed with a flair, set down before the customer on a bar that was always clean, with a bar napkin placed under the glass. Ashtrays were emptied frequently, and you always lit a gentleman or lady's cigarette with your

Zippo lighter. You were rewarded with a good hourly wage, job benefits, a sense of pride in your profession, and a nice amount of tips.

Learning all this did not happen overnight. I spent many hours under the watchful eye of the veteran bartenders before I was allowed to work a shift entirely on my own. By watching the veterans I learned the knack of making a bit of small talk after serving the customer and then taking their cue as to whether they wanted to talk or be left alone. You also learned when to join in their conversation, when to back off and leave them to their own affairs And your attention was always focused on the bar. If you stepped over to the waitress station to mix drinks for the dining room, or went to the rest room, when you returned you would automatically sweep your eyes over the bar, making sure no one was left unattended.

The craft and skill of actually making the drink was paramount. Liquor was "free-poured", that is, poured through a stainless steel pour spout with a cork base pushed into the neck of the bottle, into a jigger—a glass or stainless steel shot glass—and then dumped into the glass. Ice was always put in the glass first. Customers would have risen up and stormed out the door if you dispensed their booze by pushing a button on a automatic dispenser. After the booze you added any garnish, and finally the mix, if any. Certain cocktails, were indeed, shaken, not stirred, as James Bond often requested. Or possibly stirred, depending on the customer's preference. A Beefeater martini, dry—a drop or two of dry vermouth, straight up—stirred with ice in a shaker but served without ice in a chilled glass with an olive---was the epitome of the bartending art, your reward a satisfied customer and a generous tip. In addition to learning how to mix the drinks, you were expected to add the cost of the round up mentally as you mixed it, and ring up that total on the till. No bartender would ever dream of using the till as an adding machine.

When I enter bars nowadays and see what passes for bartending, it makes me want to weep. TVs, cell phones, talking to friends, laptops all are more important than waiting on customers. Ashtrays are no longer an issue at most bars since the smoking bans, but I am amazed at the number of times some one will set a drink down in front of me in a skein of water left by the previous customer's sweating drink glass or beer bottle. Also, evidently the cost of bar napkins has sky-rocketed because often all you will get, if you're lucky, is a grungy, used beer coaster under your drink.

None of this would have been tolerated when I learned the profession. But times change. Much is tolerated now that would not have been so in the past. Sometimes it's for the better and sometimes for the worst. You can still find places with excellent bartenders who are professionals at their work. When you do, compliment them on their skill. And tip generously.

After two years at the Nino's on Howell Avenue in

Milwaukee, Nino asked if I'd like to be the daytime manager at the new store opening in Appleton. My mother had grown up in the Fox River Valley area where Appleton is located and I had liked visiting the area when we went to see our relatives. It would be a promotion for me as well. I answered in the affirmative and prepared to move north. But before I left I learned one more important lesson.

On a cold night in January when I was bartending, an attractive woman in her twenties came in and ordered a drink. As I set her drink in front of her, she looked familiar but I could not recall the circumstances. It was a week-night, business slow enough that I could spend some time chatting with her. We soon established that we had met once some years ago, somewhere at a bar, where our respective dates had mutual friends among those people in our respective groups. She had continued to date the man she had been with, and was now married to him. I, on the other hand, was still single and liking it. Nino's on Howell was directly across from Mitchell Field, the Milwaukee airport. She had just dropped her husband off for a flight somewhere on business and decided to have a drink on her way home.

She was quite friendly, and after a couple more drinks, began to flirt a little with me. I responded, but kept in mind that often it didn't mean anything. A lot of times a woman will flirt, then pick up her purse, say a sweet good night and leave. Sometimes she was approached by other men in the bar but, although she was nice to them, they did not hang around.

"I hope you don't mind," she explained as I brought her another drink. "But I told them we were married and I'm here to see you. It eliminates so much hassle."

That was fine with me. I didn't mind being cast in the role of husband and couldn't help but wonder if there was some sort of Freudian significance attached. I decided to toss the ball back onto her side of the court. I told her the drink was on me and casually added that since I had the early shift I'd be getting off at ten thirty if it didn't get busy. She smiled and said nothing.

A friend of mine told me one time about his method to determine if he was going to get laid on a first date. He'd pick up the woman, and on the way to their destination, he would pull up in front of a drugstore. "I'm going in to buy some condoms," he would tell her as he went inside. If she was still in the car when he returned he figured it was a pretty sure thing. "Why spend all your time and money if it isn't going to pay off," was his reasoning. "After all, we do all the asking, the driving, the wining and dining. They got the easy part."

Now I didn't necessarily agree with his thought process but I could understand the logic. I felt, however, that my method was more subtle, and not quite so crude. It left room for either of the parties involved to go their separate ways with their pride and dignity intact. She knew what time I got off. If she was still there at ten thirty I would definitely sit down next to her and have a few drinks. And see where it would lead to.

It led to her apartment. She did indeed stay until I got off of work, and we had our drinks. And after an hour or so on some very pleasurable anticipatory amorous sporting that determined we had the same thing in mind, we left.

"I'll follow you," I said, breath steaming in the cold as we approached our vehicles in the parking lot.

"My apartment is really hard to find," she answered. "Why don't you ride with me and I'll bring you back."

A small warning buzz went off somewhere in my mind but, sadly, the little head was overriding anything happening in the big head. I helped her clear the frost from her windshield and we jumped in her car and took off. Her apartment was a long ways away and tucked away in a newer neighborhood of houses and small apartments. The streets had been laid out by an addle-minded designer who, convincing himself that straight lines were the enemy of the people, had created a maze of winding lanes, dead-end courts, and looping streets with names like Cherry Hill Drive, Fernwood Glen Court, and the like. The skinny, newly-planted trees with their wrapped trunks passing by the window in the yellowish glow of the street lamps stood in the deep snow like lost and abandoned children. In daylight and sober Daniel Boone would have gotten lost. In my current state of rut, and with this now-lovely creature in charge, I was too focused on what lay ahead to pay any attention to where we were going.

We got inside her apartment, she slipped a chain lock on the door, and in a matter of seconds we were naked and in her bed. It was frenzied, crazy, slightly depraved, and fantastic. After a couple of hours of mutual ecstasy we dropped off into an exhausted slumber.

I was jerked awake by a loud knocking.

"Maggie!. Maggie!" The voice was loud, echoing through the apartment, followed by the rattling of the chain lock as the door bounced against it several times.

"Shit," she hissed fiercely. "It's my husband. Get out! Get out!"

Husband? Shit, he was supposed to be on an airplane.

"Where, for the Chris sake?"

"Here. The window." She was already over to it, sliding up the sash.

Heart pounding, buck naked, I ran over to the opening, awkwardly slipped over the sill, and dropped into a foot of snow. "Christ, my clothes," I gasped but she was already gathering them up and pitching them out the window at me, calling loudly over her shoulder, "I"m coming, honey. Just a minute."

The window slid shut and I stood in the darkness along side the building. Hastily I pulled on my pants, shirt and groped in the snow until I found my shoes where they had landed some feet away. I searched desperately for my coat but it was not in sight.

Hastily I gave up looking, wanting only to get the hell away from where ever I was. Clutching my shoes, shorts and undershirt, I ran barefoot through the snow across the back yard, plunged through a snowbank, and found myself on the neighboring driveway, dimly lit by the glow of the streetlight at its entrance. Concealed in the shadow of the garage, I put on my socks and shoes and walked furtively to the street where I turned right, away from her apartment building.

I walked for what seemed like hours through that maze of streets, seeing only an endless procession of houses and apartments, shaking from the cold. I pulled my undershirt on over my dress shirt, wrapped my arms around my chest but it didn't help at all. Bitterly I cursed myself, my stupidity, my lack of my coat, my lack of a vehicle and then earnestly prayed to God that if he would deliver me from my plight I would never, never sin again. I continued to walk, searching ahead of me for some sign of a gas station, an all-night diner, any place of refuge but I knew my chances were slim to none. It was well past bar time and all the taverns were closed. And the damn area I was in wasn't likely to be home to any diners.

I began to fear for my safety. I could picture my frozen body in the light of morning, sprawled in the snow, icy and blue, and some small school girl staring at it before she runs to get her mother. I was seriously considering going up to a house and, despite the lateness of the hour, ringing the doorbell and pleading for help, when a car pulled up. It's passenger window slid down.

"Christ, buddy. You ok?" The driver peered at me with a worried frown.

He was about ten years older than me, and looked rugged and capable, dressed in a bulky work coat. I walked up to the window, but he didn't give me a chance to voice my request for help. He leaned over and opened the door. "Get in here."

I slid in gratefully, clutching my frozen fingers between my legs as I huddled on the seat. The warm interior of the car felt so good I almost wept. He looked at me.

"Why do I think this has something to do with a broad?"

I nodded, and without mentioning the cause, outlined my predicament. When I told him my car was out by Mitchell Field, he was taken aback.

"That's about 20 miles from here. Shit, I'm headed to work. What about I take you part way, you can get a cab."

I told him that would be great, thanked him profusely and sank back as he drove to an all-night gas station.

"You got money?" he queried as he dropped me off. I assured him I did, thanked him again and silently blessed him as he drove off. I entered the station where the attendant eyed me in silence as I called a cab on the pay phone. When I finally reached my apartment the sun was coming up. I went to bed and thought seriously of staying there for about a month.

I never saw her again. A week later when I came into work, a large cardboard box with only my first name on it was waiting. Inside was my coat. From that night on, over all the years and the many times I've met a woman and we left a place together, never again did I leave my car behind. Never. Ever.

And one time at a party, I picked up a lovely young lady and we decided to move on to my place. As we walked towards the street, I asked:

"Would you like to ride with me?"

"No, I'll follow you," she said, smiling sweetly. "I've found out that there isn't much I can't get out of with a blow job and my own car."

Women do have it tougher than men, no matter what my friend says.

4

ON TO APPLETON

Since I was well-versed in the Nino's operation because of my working at the Howell Avenue location, my new job as day manager in Appleton came about with little adjustment on my part. It involved making up schedules, ordering liquor and foodstuffs, acting as host during the noon lunch hour and general supervision. I would also interview and hire much of the help. I have to say, despite being single, I hired the waitresses based on experience rather than only on appearance. However, it certainly wasn't my fault if some of them were also young and attractive. Why fight the inevitable? So in due time, being young, single and evidently attractive myself, I ended up screwing quite a few of our female staff. In addition, I had a steady girlfriend in Milwaukee and also met a number of young local women not connected to Nino's. Overall, it led to a quite active sex life.

Directly across from our location on Hy 41 was a small motel called the American Motor Inn. Clean and well-kept, it was run by Ralph and Lillian S. who lived on the premises. In addition to nice rooms at a reasonable rate, it had a small bar in the lobby where Ralph would tend bar. It was a great local hangout and perfect for clandestine rondeveauxs as long as you were discreet and didn't cause trouble. I also had my apartment for those trysts when it didn't make any difference if anyone noticed who was with me. Over time, at these places, or at the various houses and apartments of the single women, I bedded a lot of women.

At work, there was Peggy, a petite, dark-eyed cutie who was the week-end bar waitress. When we would meet at her place after she got off of work, she would staunchly resist all my advances until I would get up to leave and then she'd give in and we'd end up in bed and screw the rest of the night. This happened no matter how many times we'd go to her house. Puzzled, after the first half a dozen times, I mentioned it to her. Why the struggle? She looked at me like I was crazy and denied knowing what I was talking about. Thirty minutes later we were going through the routine. I figured what the hell, it was worth it, and didn't bring it up again. But it did seem a trifle strange.

There was Shirley L., a married woman who told her husband she was working late when she was in my bed. He, sadly enough, believed her to the extent he came in to work and threatened to report us to the state for making his wife work all those extra hours. In the broadest way possible, I told him to be very sure he knew what he was talking about before doing anything foolish. After that she stopped coming to my place but that was ok with me, she was good but not great.

There was Christine, a divorced mother of five who looked barely old enough to be out of high school. During the time of our affair, her ex-husband would commit suicide by smashing his car into an enormous oak tree in the small morning hours. Also, one of her daughters, who was five years old, developed Hodgkin's Disease. Fortunately, the daughter made a recovery. Through all her problems, Christine remained hopeful and decent towards others. Eventually we drifted apart but we always felt a special bond afterward.

One of the local ladies I met was Barbie N., a cute redhead who worked days for a local record producer. At night she'd cocktail waitress at the Terrace Motor Inn and Supper Club. We rarely went out on a date. Instead I'd simply drive by her place after bar time and if her car was there, let myself inside. We liked the same things in bed and she was always fun to be naked with.

Anna's husband was an honest-to-God door-to-door bible salesman. The bibles he sold were large, elaborately decorated and embellished, and very expensive. He was very good at his job and pulled in a nice income. He was also gone from home quite a bit. Anna would let me know when she was available and we would do all those nasty things that the bible enumerated as the sure road to hell. I also would share my place and my bed with her niece from Tennessee when she'd come for a visit. Dorothy was a lively, short sweetie with long brown hair and great breasts.

There were others, so many that in time I became overwhelmed with guilt. In a fit of remorse, I wrote a letter to my girlfriend in Milwaukee saying we should break up.

But I didn't say why. I wasn't that stupid. The next night there was a knock on my door. There she stood, letter in hand, having driven from Milwaukee after right she got home from work and opened the letter. With angry tears, she told me no way, I was not going to break up with her and she never wanted to get another letter like that again. Of course, with my poor moral fiber I didn't confess to my straying. Instead I admitted it was a stupid thing to do, I was sorry, and we reconciled. And I did change my ways for a while. But then I began to backslide, and soon was back to my old tricks.

After Nino's was open for a couple of months, the Left Guard opened up. From the moment we opened we had done a thriving business at Nino's. Although we felt some concern about the impact of the Guard's opening on our business, it did not prove to be the case. It was the sixties, and although both Vietnam and civil rights were changing the country in ways no one could have ever imagined, the economy was strong and growing. Both businesses did well and thrived. And I was happy. I had a good job that paid well, plenty of women, and now a place to go on Monday nights where I could actually stand next to and maybe even chat with some of the Green Bay Packers. I had no way of knowing that, in a couple of years due to the vagaries of life, I would end up working there and get to know some of the players first-hand as they became part of the Lombardi-era legend.

5

THE LEFT GUARD

The Left Guard in Appleton was actually the third of Max's and Fuzzy's places to open. Prior to its arrival, Max had bought a bar in Manitowoc, which he re-named the Left End. Although he often stopped there, the hands-on management was left in the hands of an older couple. Fuzzy was the owner, along with partner Bill Martine, of a place in Menasha called the Left Guard. Both of these places, modest in size, had been operating as bars before Max and Fuzzy took over. Max and Fuzzy had them remodeled to reflect their Packer affiliation and both places had gone over well with their new decor and menus.

The new Left Guard, to be located in Appleton, was selected to capitalize on the success of the two smaller places and become the flag-ship operation. Built from the ground up, in a busy commercial strip on West College Avenue, it was located less than a mile from Highway 41, the double-lane highway between Appleton and Green Bay . It was large, including in its facilities a main barroom, a main dining room, kitchen, storage areas, and a large banquet room with its own bar.

It was deluxe facility. The exterior was dark wood and brick, surrounded by a large parking area. A huge green and gold, football-shaped sign with the Left Guard name dominated the front. Interior walls were of an attractive mellow earth-toned brick, accented by Packer green and gold paneling. The carpeting was Packer green. Furniture and additional trim was a dark, polished wood. Some other areas in the back were enhanced by sections of vivid red wall paneling.

As you entered the front entrance, directly ahead was a hallway. Immediately to its right was the bar room, entered and exited through two broad openings. As you walked down the hall, the coat check and restrooms were on your left, the main dining room directly ahead. After passing through the dining room, you entered another hallway. To its right lay the kitchen. On the left side of the hallway were storage areas and the employees break room. Further down the hall was the banquet hall.

The bar at The Left Guard was u-shaped. The ends of the U sides were about 20 feet in length, and stopped about eight feet from the rear wall of the bar that separated it from the dining room. Shorter bar sections then ran at a right angle from the ends of the U sides, parallel to the wall. After about 12 feet these shorter sections terminated at a couple of brick columns. About 35 bar stools stood at these sections, as well as the front part of the U, where the customers were seated or, when busy, stood.

Between the columns and the rear wall was a section of bar with no bar stools. These two lengths, called service, were used strictly by the waitresses for their drink orders. On the left side this section of bar was open to the hallway to the dining room, used by the waitresses getting drinks for the dinner guests and, after the dining room closed for the night, by the cocktail waitress working the bar. The section on the right faced out on the table and dance floor area of the bar room, and was used by additional cocktail waitresses on a busy night.

Four work stations were located behind the bar. All of them were set up to provide storage for glasses, an ice bin with a soda dispensing gun above, a glass- washing set-up and rails to hold liquor bottles, all of this equipment stainless steel. The two service work stations, since they were located next to the rear room wall, had coolers for beer and other perishables built in. On top of the coolers stood bottles of call liquors and the cash register.

The two additional work stations were located in the main part of the U, in the part of the bar was called "the point." Since no wall was there, the beer coolers were under the bar itself, the till on top. Regardless of location, the arrangement of liquor, glasses, etc. was as nearly identical as possible at all the stations, so any bartender could move to where the demand was heaviest and find himself able to work speedily, without having to re-think the logistics.

On a typical busy night there'd be at least three

bartenders working, sometimes four, one at each service station and one or two on point. "Working point" was generally tougher than working service, since the bartenders on a busy night there bore the brunt of waiting on the customers who were lined up two and three deep, often noisy, intoxicated and demanding. Generally on a busy night we'd rotate among the stations after a couple of hours so no one person had to work point all night.

The bar itself took up about half the bar room. The remaining area held cocktail tables, open traffic areas and in one corner, a small tile dance floor.

The dining room seated about ninety customers. Its menu and operation were similar to Nino's, with the broiler area located in the dining room and steaks heavily featured on the menu. Packer photos and other memorabilia covered the walls.

One of my favorite things to do while at the Left Guard was walk along the hallway leading to the banquet room in back. Along one wall huge photos ran from floor to ceiling, covering the paneling. They were those incredible, great iconic Packer photos which have now been reproduced countless times all over the sports world. There was the shot of the face of Forrest Gregg, spattered with mud, bearing that look of giving it his all as he heads for the sidelines. There was the photo of Don Chandler, foot extended high in the air the moment after he kicked the field goal that won the 1965 conference play-off against the Colts, while around him, in the dark and driving rain, the players clustered. Fuzzy stands among them, his hands clenched in prayer. And the famous Packer sweep, with Fuzzy and Jerry Kramer leading the way, Paul Hornung, with his trademark deceptively easy lope, charging behind them. And Max, making one of his great catches, body arching in the air, face drawn taut in total concentration as he hauls the ball in. Willie Wood, Herb Adderley and Elijah Pitts walking off the field together after a hard-fought game. All of those wonderful moments, stopped in time. They left me with a thrill every time I viewed them.

Within a few years of opening, it became apparent that some areas in the Guard were too small. An addition was built to the west, doubling the size of the bar room, and the banquet facility in back was also expanded. Not long after that a 60 unit motel with an indoor pool and atrium was erected next door and connected to the Guard via the bar room. It was, as they say, a match made in heaven. Now the good times could really roll.

6
MAX

Max McGee was a gifted individual. He was incredibly talented physically. At 6' 3" and 205 pounds, he played twelve seasons as a wide receiver with the Green Bay Packers, making 345 receptions while gaining 6,346 yards and scoring fifty touchdowns. During that time he also developed a reputation as the team's quipster and, as a roommate and best friend of Paul Hornung, the quintessential party animal. He also owned a quick intelligence and a great personality. His charming affability, along with an air of soft-spoken southern courtliness, made him a favorite where ever he went and in any group. And while not handsome in the Hollywood sense, his easy grin, quick wit and gallant, free-spirited manner many women found irresistible.

One afternoon he, myself and two young ladies were doing some casual barhopping in the Appleton area. At one of our stopping places we began to play Foosball, a game kind of like one dimensional soccer. The mechanics are simple, and its apparatus is wholly without any mechanical or electronic gadgetry. Compared to today's video games, it is akin to the horse and buggy as opposed to a modern automobile. However, it's still a popular game today in homes, bars, college unions, and the like. It's played on a small table about 2 by 4 feet with 10" sides, by either two or four players. Shafts of polished steel pass through the table sides, with handles on the outside. These shafts spin freely. Inside the table plastic or metal humanoid figures are fixed to the shafts, with their "feet," one inch in width, located about one-half inch above the table surface when the man is upright. There are eight shafts, with plastic handles attached four to a side on alternating shafts. At each end is an opening about six inches wide, representing the scoring net. In the center of each side is another opening where a ball about the size of a ping pong ball is dropped to begin play.

The players stand on either side, drop a ball through the hole when it's their turn, and play begins. By spinning and twisting the shafts with their hands, they then can smack the ball back and forth on the table top, hoping to get the ball into the goal and score. Like many things with simple dynamics, the execution can be complex. A good foosball player can fire the balls with incredible speed, use back-spin and precise ball contact to send the balls at any angle across the table, be adept at blocking techniques, and generally have a myriad of other fancy techniques in his or her foosball arsenal. Some players become so addicted to the game that they show up to play wearing gloves, carrying cans of WD-40 to lubricate the shafts.

I wasn't that much of a fanatic but did consider myself a pretty good player. This foolish notion was further strengthened that afternoon by two things: a couple of hours already spent drinking cocktails, and myself and my partner beating Max and his partner a several times.

Max, with that incredible hand-eye coordination he possessed was, of course, excellent at any game of skill. However, always gracious, he was playing at about one-quarter speed that afternoon, something I failed to realize in my alcohol-fueled flush of victory. After listening to me shoot off my mouth one time too many, he turned to his partner.

"What do you say, Candace? Should we give him a lesson?"

She happily agreed.

He, with Candace contributing, then proceeded to kick it into overdrive. Smack! Smack! Smack! Smack! Hands a blur of motion, slouched casually at the table, a Camel hanging from his lips, he slammed in shot after shot, winning the game. In spite of realizing I had unleashed his cheerful wrath, I demanded another match, then another, gamely trying to recover, trying to get control of the balls, trying to block his shots, always a second too slow as I grabbed at the handles. My partner, at this point, wisely retreated to the bar, leaving me to face my doom on my own. After soundly getting my ass kicked several times I finally gave up. By then we were all out of breath, laughing, and I was even enjoying my demise. After all, as Johnny Lang sings in *Rack 'Em Up* 'It ain't no disaster in getting beat by the master.' Max played the last game standing with his back to the table so I could salvage a pity victory.

I saw the same thing happen a lot. Whether pool, dice, pinball, cards, any game of skill or chance, Max approached it with an air of easy nonchalance. But his great physicality combined with a quick intelligence almost always gave him an edge. When I mentioned it once to Paul Hornung, McGee's close friend and Packer room mate, he laughed.

"You've got him figured out. He's taken a lot of money off of a lot of people with that aw shucks routine of his. He's damn competitive when he wants to be."

Max smoked Camel cigarettes at the time. They came in the traditional soft pack, with its tin foil package secured at the top by a blue tax stamp. Everyone on the face of the earth opened a cigarette pack by tearing away the one-third of the foil next to the stamp. One of his favorite tricks was to be talking to someone at the bar, pull out a fresh pack, tear it open, and tap the bottom edge on the bar rail. A cigarette would then pop neatly through the air and he'd catch it between his lips. All the while Max would still be talking. It didn't work every time, but generally more often than not. It was an impressive trick, and he often used it while chatting up some lovely lady.

While at the bar at the Left Guard, Max would often get involved in dice games. He would sometimes do the trick of, prior to his shake, tossing the dice cup in the air where it would tumble around a couple of times before he'd catch it and slam it on the bar. Centrifugal force kept the dice in the cup while it was spinning. It was a neat trick, and not for the faint of heart. If you screwed up, the dice cup often ended up in the wash sink behind the bar, the five dice scattered high and low around the barroom, and a goodly heaping of ridicule and catcalls upon your head. With his great physical ability, however, Max never muffed the trick. A couple of times I even saw him catch the cup behind his back.

One of his other physical attributes was revealed to me in a rather interesting manner. One evening he and I spent a nice night on the town accompanied by two lovely ladies whom I shall call Nadine and Mary Beth. As the evening wound down, we ended up at Max's apartment in Neenah, after stopping to pick up my car where I had left it at the Guard in Appleton. Max, who was single at the time, had purchased a two story four unit apartment building and had remodeled the top floor, combining the two units into one. To accommodate his size, he had enlarged the living area and furnished it with big, comfortable furniture. He also made the one bedroom bigger for his king-size bed. It was roomy, comfortable bachelor pad, nicely furnished but not lavish.

After a couple of drinks, he and Mary Beth disappeared to try out his king-size bed. Left on our own, Nadine and myself made do by dimming the lights, taking off all our clothes and stretching out on the plush carpet. In one corner a stereo console sat, playing romantic LPs, which were also piped into Max's bedroom. Lost in the throes of passion, we unknowingly wiggled ourselves over in front of it where we were proceeded to get it on.

We were locked in the missionary position when she tapped my shoulder and murmured "Max."

A little pissed off, I replied, "No, I'm Bob."

No, she whispered and gestured with her head. I looked up and indeed, Max was standing in the room. Naked. Wrapped in our amorous rapture we had failed to notice that the music had ended. Max explained to me later that, after waiting for us to start the music again and it not happening, he had assumed we'd left. He slipped out of bed and came into the room to do it himself. He rounded the corner and saw us on the floor, between him and the stereo. He paused, thought about going back for his robe, but since we'd already seen him and he'd seen us and since everyone was naked, and, basically since all he could really see anyway was my "ugly ass" as he put it, he discarded the idea. He came over, stepped quickly over us, and in a moment the music began. He passed over us again, politely murmured "excuse me" and exited.

"Classy guy," I commented as I got back to business.

"Yeah." Nadine agreed, tightening her arms around me. "And he's really hung, too."

7
FUZZY

In his wonderful book *Instant Replay* Jerry Kramer recounts how at the start of the training camp in Green Bay in 1967, Fuzzy Thurston hurt his knee and had to sit out a couple of days. It was in July, with the temperature above 90 degrees, and Vince Lombardi was putting the team through an agonizing series of grass drills, to the point where several players were keeling over from heat exhaustion. At the edge of the field ice was kept for treating fractures and sprains. At opportune moments, Fuzzy would sneak some ice from the coolers, put it under his sweat jacket and hobble out onto the field on his bad knee and give slivers and bits of it to his teammates. Kramer said that it was one of the "sweetest things he'd ever tasted."

It didn't surprise me when I read this. I can honestly say that in all the times I ever had anything to do with Fuzzy, he was always good to virtually anyone he met. If you were a friend, he'd go out of his way to help you out.

Keith M. was the bar manager at the Appleton Guard and my boss. He and his wife, myself and my girlfriend at the time, had made plans for a vacation in Florida. Before we'd left we'd made arrangements to stay at a condominium on Marco Island. Part of a larger development that included a golf course as well as single family houses, the condo was owned by Doc Lehman, an Appleton dentist and a friend, and a frequent customer at the Guard. The condo was located in a building of a dozen units, most of which had been purchased by people from Appleton. Fuzzy owned one and, I believe, was also a part-owner of the building. Like today, when not occupied by the owner, the units were available for rent.

Upon arrival we got a key from the building manager and, toting our bags, took the elevator up to the unit on the second floor. But as we unlocked the door, we were confronted by a rather startled stranger inside. Yes, we were at Unit 12. No, he didn't know anything about our arrival. He had rented it for the next two weeks. We went back downstairs and we're trying to get it sorted out with the manager when Fuzzy walked through the lobby. At this time Fuzzy and Max and other investors had opened up several more Left Guards, including one in Miami. Although Fuzzy still came into the Appleton store, he often was now absent, supervising the other locations as well.

"Hello, boys. What are you doing here?" he asked in surprise.

We were explaining our dilemma when he interrupted.

"Grab your bags. Come with me."

He ushered us down the hall and unlocked the door to a unit.

"This is my place," he said as we entered. "You can stay here as long as you like."

We couldn't do that, we protested. Where would he stay?

He had to go to Miami tomorrow anyway, he explained. Tonight he'd stay with Jim Carter. Handing us the key, he added, "And I'll be back for you guys at 7. There's a party tonight at a woman's house who was married to the richest hog farmer in Alabama. It'll be a good time."

It was. The house was a new, luxurious two bedroom ranch design located on the golf course. We trooped in and Fuzzy introduced us to our hostess, a forty something blonde with a trim figure and nice smile. When we complimented her on her lovely home, she laughed.

"Thank my ex," she said cheerfully. "He's the biggest hog farmer in Alabama. He ran off with his secretary because she had big tits. Well, I hope he still likes them because they cost him plenty."

Jimmy Carter, currently the middle-linebacker for the Packers, a Packer wide receiver who's name escapes me, and a couple of Tampa Bay players were also there. Several neighboring couples also showed up, and some women friends of our hostess. As darkness fell an alligator or two came crawling out on the green but kept their distance, although they did raise their snouts from time to time to catch the aroma of the steaks sizzling on the grill. The booze was good and plentiful. It was a fine, mellow evening and everyone had a good time.

As I stepped over to the bar to freshen my drink, I happened to overhear Fuzzy and Jim Carter talking out on the patio. Fuzzy was asking Jim if he could stay with him at his condo until Friday, when they were both due in Miami.

"No problem, Fuzz," Jim answered.

This was a Sunday night. I realized then that Fuzzy saying he had to go to Miami tomorrow when he gave us his condo was pure fabrication. He'd said it simply to make us feel at ease, so we wouldn't feel like we were putting him out. And later that evening, when Keith and I tried to give him some money for rent, he refused to take it. "Just replace any of the booze you drink," he laughed.

And that was Fuzzy. He was generous to a fault. When he'd be at the bar shaking dice in a high-stakes game, he'd often push the pot over to whoever was working when he won. "This is for my bartenders," he'd say. And anyone working for him knew he was a soft touch, almost always willing to help you out in a jam. I think in later years, when, because of changing times, business began to drop off, it hurt him financially to a greater degree than necessary since he just couldn't get tough on people who owed him money.

In Dave Marannis's great book on Vince Lombardi, he
devotes a number of pages to Fuzzy and his life, both
during and prior to his career as a Packer. I learned that
Fuzzy had grown up in a large family, his father had died
when he was still young, and it had been tough financially.
His actions appeared to me to be those of someone who
has never forgotten their roots and, in Fuzzy's case, his
early experiences made him caring and compassionate
about other people. Not everyone reacts in that way.

Like Max, he was also very physically talented. Unlike
Max, who was tall and lanky, Fuzzy appeared short and
stocky. But his stocky appearance was due to his
musculature. He was very strong. Occasionally, on a bet, he
would drop down on the bar room floor and do fifty one-
handed push-ups. Another time I saw him single-handed
wrestle a refrigerator in place back in the kitchen. Despite
his bulky appearance, he was also very quick and agile.

Fuzzy also liked to have fun, and was almost always in
a good mood. He liked being in the bar, talking and joking
with friends. He would sometimes do crazy things.
Eventually a motel was built next to the Left Guard, and a
walkway connected the two buildings. At the motel interior
was a large atrium with an indoor pool. During the festive
nights leading to the 1000 Yard Club banquet, at bar time
Fuzzy would unplug the jukebox, roll it out of the bar and
into the pool area. He'd then come behind the bar and grab
the rolls of quarters out of the change box to plug it with.
Finally, a portable bar would be rolled in the pool area as

well, so the party could last until dawn. Since virtually every room surrounding the pool was rented to persons there for the banquet, it worked out fine. And the following day Fuzzy would seek out whichever bartenders had worked and give them a generous bonus.

Other times he and his cronies at the bar would go to great lengths to pull a practical joke. One evening a stranger stopped in, and, after a few drinks, worked himself over to where he was integrating himself into the group of regulars gathered at the bar. He bought a round--always a good way to break the ice—and introductions were made all around. The stranger, after chatting a bit, then made the comment that his watch had stopped working. "Heck," Fuzzy assured him. "Dick is a jeweler. He can fix that in no time."

Before the man could protest, Fuzzy slipped the watch off the stranger's wrist and handed it to Dick, one of the regulars. Now everyone there knew Dick O. was a jewelry salesman, not a jeweler. They watched to see what would happen. Dick picked up on the joke without missing a beat. He sat down at the bar and using a small pocket knife and a couple of bar picks, took the watch apart. He hummed and hawed, poking at its innards. The stranger began to look worried. Those standing behind him traded furtive smiles. A small spring shot up into the air and disappeared. "Shit," Dick commented. The others pushed in closer. "How's it looking?" someone asked after some minutes had gone by. Dick shook his head sadly. He unfolded a bar napkin and gathered up the myriad of tiny springs, wheels, shafts, crystal and the other remaining parts. Placing them on the napkin, he folded it up and handed it to the owner.

"Here. I can't fix it."

The whole group erupted in laughter at the shocked and baffled expression on the man's face. Just as he began to get angry, Fuzzy slapped him on the back and bought him a drink, declaring he was a good sport and one of the gang. Dick went out to his car and returned with a new watch, which they presented to their victim. He accepted it happily, stayed late into the evening, got pleasantly drunk, and, thrusting his arm in front of whoever would listen, proudly show them the "watch that Fuzzy Thurston gave me."

One time, however, Fuzzy was not a happy camper. Someone had stolen the Packer's playbook out of his unlocked car. He had to tell Coach Lombardi, who was furious. The police were also notified, and the word was quickly put out that whoever had taken it would find it wise to return it immediately, no questions asked. The culprit was a free-spirited Left Guard regular named Elsie, who had done it in a moment of pique when a Packer had spurned her offer of affection. Up until she swiped the playbook her sole claim to local notability was that she tooled around town in one of the famous Mary Kay pink Cadillacs, which she had earned selling their products. She knew almost immediately that she was in trouble but was afraid to admit she took it until she heard about the amnesty offer. Then she tearfully returned it, and all was forgiven.

Fuzzy was married to Sue, his high school sweetheart, and he doted on her and their small children. She would come in often, sometimes bringing the children, and the family would sit down together for dinner. Sue was a good match for Fuzzy, she always seemed as easy going as he was. More importantly, she somehow was able to tolerate his craziness when it got out of hand. All of the help liked her.

One time Fuzzy ventured into capitalizing on his fame as a sports legend. He appeared in some print ads in various men's magazines for Usher's Green Stripe scotch, a brand that few drinkers had ever heard of. The ads showed Fuzzy in his Packers' helmet, with his tough game-day face on. The ad said something like "After a rough game I like to relax with the smooth taste of Usher's Green Stripe scotch." In return Fuzzy got some cash and a large number of cases of Green Stripe. Fuzzy put the cash in his pocket. We put the Green Stripe in the bar rail and poured it as our bar scotch. The only problem was the scotch tasted god-awful. Customers would order a scotch and soda and we'd set it up. After one sip, they'd say, "What the hell brand of scotch is that? It tastes like piss. Take it away and give me a J&B."

Fuzzy was stymied. He felt compelled to honor his end of the bargain, even though he couldn't stand the taste of it either. He solved the dilemma by giving away most of it, making a big deal out of it. "Hey, here, lemme give you a bottle of Green Stripe. Best scotch there is," he'd announce grandly as he presented the unsuspecting recipient with his free gift. We eventually got rid of the remaining cases by using it at the bars set up for banquets and other occasions where the clientele's palettes were less discriminating..

8

Good Times at the Bar

While there were always plenty of available women hanging around the Guard, the Packer players' relationships with them were not always an endless succession of wild nightly parties, with rampant sex. Certainly there were some of those but it was far from a continuous orgy. For one thing, during the football season, the players had only two nights of the week off, Sunday night after a game, and Monday nights. The rest of the week their tom cat actions were restricted by a ten pm team curfew. While some players like Max McGee and Paul Hornung became famous for violating curfew, in reality it happened only rarely. And, if the team had played on the road, the players spent Sunday night traveling back, arriving too late to Green Bay to do much except go home to bed. So often it was a single night of the week that they were able to make the ladies happy.

And if a lovely lady was fortunate enough to form a quasi-permanent relationship with a player, it was based on the tacit understanding that in all likelihood it would end when the football season ended, when most of the players returned to their home towns and cities, rejoining families and often a home town sweetheart. In the interim, there would be a lot of nights alone, waiting for the phone to ring, while she waited for her man. Still, the rewards could be fulfilling. The prestige, the thrill, the bragging rights of dating a Green Bay Packer, could go a long way in making up for any of the difficulties. A few of the women adopted a pragmatic approach. I dated a women for a while who was also going out with Paul Hornung. By this time Paul had retired from playing, and while he still frequented the area, he would often be gone for long periods. The lady, a lovely, gray-eyed beauty, told me frankly after a couple of our dates that, while she was quite happy to continue to see me, when Paul called her he would have priority. After while we drifted apart but I always appreciated her honesty.

Sometimes too, the players themselves were not always looking for a party. I recall on many Monday nights seeing Packer center Ken Bowman, running backs Donny Anderson and John Brockington, receiver Boyd Dowler and other Packer packers passing hours in quiet conversation with various women, whether dating them or not. In spite of their profession, or perhaps even more so because of it, at times they seemed curiously vulnerable, a touch lonely, needing a caring companion to help them deal with the same kind of devils that perhaps plagued us lesser mortals.

The women themselves were a mixed group. Single, divorced, sometimes married, of all ages and shapes, whether beauties or of lesser physical quality, they all liked to have fun. This was during the decade when the pill became readily accessible. Mini-skirts had swept the nation and were now common attire, and feelings of peace and free love were everywhere, in the music, in the news, on all the TV shows. Old morals and standards had crumbled and sexual freedom, along with a looser attitude towards many other things shaping our lives, slipped in to fill the void. In spite of the pall cast by the war in Vietnam, times were good, and people wanted to be out, be seen, be dressed up, go a little crazy and have a good time. That the Green Bay Packers were at the time the kings of professional football, giving everyone something to cheer about on game days, only added to the party atmosphere. So, while not every night was a bacchanalian revel, any time the Packers were at the Left Guard, a general air of festivity and animation would quickly take shape. A lot of good-natured fun and foolishness prevailed.

A while back I read that someone had produced a play based on the life of Vince Lombardi. I have not seen it but would think it is a worthwhile effort. However, I've always felt that Broadway has missed the boat on the story of the Lombardi era Packers. To me it's a natural for a musical. Think about it. To start you have a wide range of classic characters: Lombardi, the gruff, crusty father figure who turns boys into men. Paul Hornung, the handsome, gifted golden boy running back that women fight over. Ray Nitchke, the tough guy with a chip on his shoulder from growing up homeless on the mean streets of a big city. Max, the devil-may-care party boy. Fuzzy and Jerry

Kramer, the stocky, determined guys who make the plays that make the other players heroes. Bart Starr, the strait-laced, dedicated quiet man with father issues. The grizzled old locker room trainer who gives the boys tips on what to do to play better. For the women, you have the ditzy cheerleader with the heart of gold, the sorority queen who falls for the golden boy running back, the poor, drab little girl next door who dreams of a romance with a Packer player, the football Annies who chase after all the players. And so on. Combine these characters and you have countless romantic plot lines.

For the musical numbers, hell, most of the work is done. If you can't figure out choreography based on football formations, you'd better go back to picking corn in Iowa. For example, just take the defensive backfield quartet of Bobby Jeter, Herb Adderly, Willie Wood and Tom Brown. Line them up, cue the orchestra, and you got an opening number. Another number could be based on the legendary Packer sweep, Jerry and Fuzzy charging downstage, Hornung close behind. Max racing up the aisle to catch a Bart Starr pass. High stepping cheer leading routines set to music, gala colors, flashing lights. The Packer marching band playing rousing fight songs. The Packers partying at the Left Guard on their Monday nights off, a rock band blasting music.

And drama? Once again, most of the work is done. What could be more dramatic than the true story of how Lombardi in a single season turned the Packers from a league joke into a championship team. What about Hornung's suspension from playing because of gambling? Hornung and McGee incurring Lombardi's wrath by breaking curfew the night before a big game? The heartbreak of the old veteran player who's career ends because of injury just before the championship game. The soft-spoken quarterback who finally gains the respect of his teammates and, more importantly, of his father when he proves himself a champion in the true sense of the word. The young cocky rookie who finally gains acceptance when he eschews his own pursuit of glamor for the good of the team. The second-string player who finally makes it into the line up and marries the poor little girl next door and they live happily ever after.

It's all there, folks. And when a Broadway producer puts it all together and it's a smash, remember, you first read about it here. But I digress.

Herb Adderley, the all-pro left cornerback of the Packers, was a regular at the Left Guard. He often would come in on Sunday night, after a home game. He was an exceptionally sharp dresser. Sometimes he would be joined by his teammates from the Packer defensive backfield, Bobby Jeter and Willie Wood. It was always fun to wait on them, as they were cheerful and gregarious, tipped well, and were very gracious towards everyone.

After Max retired in 1967, Bob Long, a 1964 draft pick from Wichita State, stepped up to take his place at wide receiver. During his time playing behind Max, the two had become friends. Long had gone to school in Kansas and hung around with two brothers who had begun to sell pizzas out of a tiny restaurant close to the college. They named it The Pizza Hut. By the time Long became a Packer, the brothers had opened up numerous locations in and around Kansas, and were reaching out to establish other franchise areas. Bob invested in the company, along with Max and Fuzzy, and a Pizza Hut was built on property adjoining the Left Guard.

Later in his football career, Jeter was traded to the Chicago Bears. For a while after he left, he continued his relationship with a woman from the Green Bay area named Janice. Bob Long, when the Packers and Bears played, would line up against Jeter, whose job was to defend against him. Prior to running the play, Long related later to listeners at the Left Guard, he would describe in hasty yet lurid and obscene detail some totally fictitious story involving Lynn, in an effort to distract Jeter from his game.

With its Packer connections and location next to the Left Guard, as well as a tasty product, Pizza Hut quickly became the after bar-time hang out for the Guard's clientele. Later a Kentucky Fried Chicken store opened up next to the Pizza Hut. Paul Hornung was an early investor in Kentucky Fried and it was rumored he had made a lot of money by getting in on the ground floor. In time the cooks at these three places—the Left Guard, Pizza Hut and Kentucky Fried—would get heartily sick of eating their own product and surreptitiously sneak into each other's places through the back doors during their breaks to eat the other business's offerings. All on the house, of course. Professional courtesy.

Dave Robinson, the left-side linebacker who had a great career in Green Bay, also would stop into the Guard. One Sunday night, after he had played an exceptionally good game against the Bears, I greeted him as he approached the bar.

"Hey Dave. How you doing?"

"Bob," he replied, "I'm so high I can see my house from here. And I haven't had a single drink yet."

I guess Dave was high on life, as they say.

Robinson was one of a group of Packer players who came into the Guard the evening after the famous 1967 Ice Bowl game, when the Packers defeated the Dallas Cowboys on Starr's last minute quarterback sneak. It was a trifle unusual in that all of us non-players present, who had either attended or watched the game on TV, were expecting the players to be really fired up and celebrating. But they were clustered together at several tables, generally happy but subdued in their behavior, drinking quietly and keeping to themselves. In retrospect, they were probably pretty well exhausted, perhaps wanting to simply relax and savor their victory. Bart Starr was with them but left around ten o'clock. Mary M., the cocktail waitress reported that while there he had drank two brandys and sweet soda. This was considered an indication that the Pack was indeed celebrating since Starr drank about as often as the Pope chewed snuff. After he left, the other players fired up a bit and the evening ended on a lively note.

On another occasion Jerry Kramer was visiting the Guard. In addition to Jerry and Fuzzy being friends over the years, by now they'd become famous as the pulling guards who bowled over defenders when the Packers ran their sweep. Kramer had also thrown the block against Jethro Pugh that enabled Starr to score in the famous Ice Bowl against Dallas. He and Fuzzy were drinking and having a good time with a crowd of regulars gathered round. Somehow the talk got around to when Jerry kicked place kicks for the Packers. After the fifth game of the 1962 season, Paul Hornung, who normally kicked for the Packers, injured his knee. Kramer, who had kicked in high school, stepped in and did a good job. He was a straight-legged kicker which was typical at that time. However, he had no follow-through. It was a joke in the locker room that he'd walk up to the ball-one-two-three-and boink. After Fuzzy loudly explained Jerry's technique to the crowd in the barroom, he and Jerry decided to demonstrate. An area was cleared and Fuzzy knelt, taking on the role of the ball holder. There was an imaginary hike, Fuzzy placed the imaginary ball down, Jerry, in an abbreviated fashion due to space constraint, did the one-two-three steps and boink. Of course in no time at all the crowd picked up on it and Jerry and Fuzzy had to repeat the maneuver several times, while the crowd chanted *one-two-three* as Jerry stepped, and then *boink* as he kicked, then whooping and hollering, applauding frenziedly as they threw their arms in the air to signal he'd scored.

Another Packer I happened to spend some time with was Chester Marcol, the Green Bay place kicker from 1972 to 1980, after Don Chandler retired. During the seventies, I was going out with a sweet lady from the area, Sharon P. Sharon shared an apartment with Lynn B., who had been married to one of the wealthy sons of a family from Neenah whose family had made its fortune in the paper industry. Both Green bay and Appleton were home to some of the biggest names in the paper business, with companies such as Kimberly-Clark, Begstrom Papers, and Appleton Papers operating paper mills alongside the Fox River. Lynn, now single, had met Chester and they hit it off. Even though Lynn and Sharon lived together, she and I never socialized with Lynn and Chester too much. I recall going out on one or two double dates but that was about it. Most of my time with Chester was spent mornings when we'd meet in the kitchen of the apartment. Our ladies had already gotten up and gone to work. He and I would drink coffee and just sit and talk. Chester was good-sized but he didn't have the brawny athletic build typical of a football player of the day. With his boyish face, short curly brown hair, and full cheeks, he lacked the air of menace that some of his teammates projected on or off the field. He was friendly and outgoing, and we'd talk about how the team was doing, what the next game might be like and so on. Otherwise we talked about our respective ladies, what we'd been doing, movies we'd seen, and so on.

Chester had lived in Poland until he was 14. Sharon had a lengthy Polish last name with those extra vowels and consonants typical of the language. I regularly mangled it when I pronounced it and she herself said it in a simplified, Americanized manner. However, Chester would pronounce it with all of its Polish accents and inflections, and would always greet her this way. It did sound rather elegant when he said it. One night late, after a night out, the four of us spent over an hour in the wee morning hours gathered in the living room, drinking copiously while Chester tried to teach me the "correct," or rather, Polish way, to pronounce her last name. From there we moved on to other Polish words and all of us got involved. Between the booze we'd consumed and our insincere attempts, we naturally mangled the pronunciations. Chester feigned irritation, then gave us still more difficult words to attempt. We ended up laughing hysterically at our foolishness and staggered off to bed. It was one of the funnier nights of my life.

I was no longer living in the Appleton area when Chester had the proudest moment of his football career. But I saw it on TV. During a game with the Chicago Bears, in overtime, his game-winning field goal attempt was blocked. The ball hit the ground, bounced back into his arms and he ambled into the end zone, wining the game with a touchdown. Bart Starr, now the Packer coach, awarded Chester the game ball afterward in the locker room and he broke into proud tears. Later on, after his playing career ended, he struggled through some terribly difficult times in his life, fighting with drug and alcohol addicition. But I remember him best as the quiet guy I chatted with over coffee in Lynn's kitchen.

Bar business during the day generally consisted of a quick flurry of activity making drinks for the lunch crowd and then quieting down until about four o'clock when the after-work crowd would start to arrive. One afternoon, during this lull, an attractive woman in her early thirties came in by herself and ordered a drink. I made a little small talk and then Jim W., a Packer player who was on injured reserve but still mobile, came in and sat down across from her. He'd stopped in a number of times while getting over a pulled hamstring, never drinking more than a couple of beers, mostly just idling away the time after his bouts of physical therapy. I turned my attention to stocking some bar supplies and let things progress without me. A little while later he moved over beside her and after another hour they got up and left through the door going to the motel. Shortly after the phone rang. It was Mandy, the desk clerk at the motel.

"Bob, is there a woman in there, about 30ish, probably by herself?"

"She was here. What's up?"

"Well, the cops just called. They've been calling all the motels trying to find her. I told them she checked in a couple of hours ago. It's a fake name. She's been downtown buying stuff with bad checks. And they said at a couple of places she's been shoplifting. They asked me to I ring her room but no one answered. I thought she might be in the bar. They're coming out to get her."

"Shit. Not good. Jim W. just left with her. It looked like they were going to her room."

"Well, there was no answer when I rang." He paused. "But they could still be in there."

Definitely. Doing an afternoon matinee and not stopping for the distraction of a phone call. Now I was pretty sure Jim was single but it still would not go over well with the Packer staff to read in the newspapers that he was caught in a motel room with a woman who was getting arrested for theft. "What's the room number?"

He gave it to me. I got a hold of the lone waitress on duty in the afternoon and asked her to watch the bar for a few minutes. I ran down the hall to the fugitive's room and knocked. No answer. I tried again. Still no answer. "Jim," I said as loudly as I dared. "This is Bob the bartender. You need to leave. Now. I'm not goofing around."

I returned to the bar, feeling I had done what I could. If he was in the room I was counting on him knowing that I wouldn't be banging on the door if it wasn't serious. And hopefully he'd take off alone.

The cops arrived within fifteen minutes and, when there was no answer to their calling out, had Mandy open the door. The fugitive was still inside, pretending to be talking a nap. Alone. They took her into custody and left. A half hour later my phone rang again. It was Jim, calling from a bar in Green Bay, wondering what the hell was going on. I explained and he thanked me profusely. No problem. Just part of my job.

The motel was a Midway Motor Lodge, one of three built in Wisconsin and operated by three partners. It often figured into the craziness that went on after bar time. The rooms surrounded an indoor pool and its atrium, and had sliding glass patio doors onto the pool area. When the occupants wanted privacy, heavy drapes were drawn in the room. On one occasion, during a particular raucous party at poolside, a very pretty female occupant pulled open the drapes of her room and proceeded to tantalize the males by doing a cute little dance while holding a towel in front of her naked body. What she failed to realize was she had chosen a hand towel rather than a bath towel, and while it covered her breasts nicely, it stopped short at her waist. She falsely assumed the enthusiastic response she was getting was due to her cute, provocative dance. She stumbled upon the truth when some spoil sport, a woman passing by outside the room, pointed down. She looked down, discovering her shortcoming. With a shriek, she abruptly turned and fled back out of sight. A moment later the drapes were abruptly jerked closed. Outside the applause went on for several minutes, but no encore was forthcoming.

On another occasion one evening a bed appeared on a

stair landing between the motel floors, complete with sheets, blanket and pillows. How it came to be there was a total mystery. But the next morning a maid called the front desk to report it was occupied by a couple and should she wake them up? When the irate desk clerk arrived the hallway sleepers explained to that they had left the bar at closing and had come across the bed on the way to their room. Feeling tired, they figured why go any further.

Another time a salesman reported he went to his room late one evening and, when he opened the door, found its bed occupied by a Packer defensive lineman known for his enormous size and mean disposition, and a woman about one/third the player's size. The salesman wisely retreated and reported the problem to the front desk. The desk clerk, deciding it was wise to let a sleeping, mean-as-a-junk-yard-dog, 280 pound professional football player lie, gave the salesman another room to sleep in and billed his previous room to the Left Guard. How the mix-up ever came about was never determined and nothing else ever came of it.

On another occasion a good-looking black-haired woman in her mid-twenties came in early on a Thursday night. She was nicely shaped but had an air of edginess about her. After a couple of drinks, she looked around at the general lack of activity at the bar and asked:

"Any Packer players come in here?"

I explained it was generally only on Monday nights. She nodded, finished her drink. "I'll be back then," and exited out the door leading to the motel..

True to her word, next Monday evening she walked into the bar. A goodly bunch of Packers had shown up, along with a lot of customers, and we were very busy. She had spent some careful time on her hair and make-up and, in a sexy red outfit with a low-cut top, she was looking good. Within a few minutes she had a number of eager males approach her. For the next hour she laughed and smiled, accepted drinks when her glass was empty, and worked at drawing in her prey, a good-looking Packer linebacker whom I'll call Jerry that she had singled out. They left soon after, few people noticing as they pushed their way through the crowd to exit together towards the motel.

A couple of hours later they came back. Jerry ordered drinks for both of them and stood next to her but they barely spoke. In a little while she moved over to where some other players were clustered at the bar. Shortly she was in their midst, laughing and chatting with them, while they gathered around her. Jerry remained at the spot she had vacated and paid no attention, a slight bemused smile on his face. Within a half hour she again left, this time with a different Packer. After an hour or so I looked up to see she had again returned, this time alone. She immediately went over to the players and once again integrated herself in their midst. By this time Jerry had rejoined the other players but his presence didn't seem to phase her at all. She started to flirt with yet another player. But then she committed a tactical error. She got up to go to the Ladies Room and Jerry began talking. I stepped over to where the players stood to eavesdrop.

"She's fuckin' crazy," Jerry was telling the others. "We screwed like a couple of maniacs but it was like she was pissed off about something. When it was over she was up and dressed like a flash. 'C'mon let's go back to the bar,' she said. Bam, she's out the door while I've barely got my socks on. But I figure what the hell. Then we came back and she picked up Robbie. I don't know where the hell he is. I think she's trying to pick us off one by one."

When she returned she encountered a much cooler reception. The players were no longer flattered by her presence, and made it obvious, pretty much ignoring her. While her actions might have worked at a party of horny frat boys, these were Packer players, a prideful bunch used to being number one and who generally had their pick of any woman they desired. They did not find it necessary to take third or fourth offerings from any one woman. In addition, the woman appeared to be on some personal vendetta for reasons she alone understood. This held the potential for way too much trouble.

She quickly picked up on the mood and flounced off. Realizing her hustle was exposed, she chose to lower her sights. Within minutes she zeroed in on a new target at the bar, a drunken salesman who could scarcely believe his good fortune. Soon I could see her leading him away towards the motel, an unsuspecting lamb with a silly smile on his face. I almost felt sorry for him.

Incredibly enough, she returned one more time, again alone. I began to wonder if she was silently slaughtering these guys and stashing their body in the dumpster out back. By this time it was bar time, the lights were up and the crowd thinning out. She motioned me over and asked for a drink. I told her it was too late and I could no longer serve her. Without another word, quick as lightning, she reached across the bar and stuck her room key into my shirt pocket. Then she got up and went back to her room.

I finished closing up and left. Outside as I walked to my car I tossed the key into the dumpster. The I went over to the Pizza Hut and got something to eat before I went home to bed. A week later Jerry came into the bar and said that the night before, a Sunday night after a home game, he had seen her again, this time at a bar in Green Bay, hustling some of the Packer players there. He added that he'd heard of some groupies trying to screw an entire rock-and-roll band but he'd never run into one who was trying to do a whole football team.

Maybe she's just doing the first string players, I said and he laughed. Whoever she was and whatever her reasons, no one ever discovered.

One of the waitresses who worked the dining room was a tall, leggy brunette with huge eyes whom I'll call Lily. The contrast between her cute baby doll face and those long sexy legs drove me crazy, causing a mix of lustful yet ingenuous thoughts of seduction. I had a crush on her that became apparent. Unfortunately she was married, so although she sometimes did a little innocent flirting with me, she treated me with the kindness that older women often use on a suffering schoolboy in an identical position. I took it all with good grace. What I found somewhat puzzling was the fact that her husband was, to put it bluntly, a really nerdy guy. He was short, with a roundish face and heavy black glasses. He kind of waddled when he walked and had a mawkish manner of speaking. He managed a supermarket and once when he came into the Guard to speak to her about something, he actually had a long white apron on under his jacket. Not cool at all. They were a most unlikely couple but for a long while she dutifully stayed on the straight and narrow.

However, one evening a group of Packer players came into the dining room and sat at one of her tables. The rest, as they say, is history. Lily tumbled hard for one of their number, a lanky good-looking, back-up defensive player. An affair started and for a long time they managed to be so discreet that no one was aware of it. But as these things always do, word got out. And, as it also always seems, when her nerdy husband Stanley finally figured it out, he was the last to know.

After months of her coming home later and later at night, telling him a multitude of stories about working later, helping out a stranded girlfriend, car trouble, having a few drinks with the girls, he finally became suspicious. He waited in his car a discreet distance from the Left Guard and followed her when she left. She met her lover and the two of them drove in their separate cars to an apartment that a friend had been letting them use for their trysts. Poor Stanley confronted the irrefutable evidence of his wife's unfaithfulness as he watched the two of them, giggling and embracing, trading kisses as they went inside. He drove to a nearby bar and got quietly drunk. Then he drove back to the apartment and slowly drove into the side of the Packer player's car. Then he backed up and did it again. And again. And several more times. Then he worked on the front end, mashing in the grill, before moving around and busting up the taillights and rear fender areas. Then he drove off.

Ensconced in a back upper apartment, locked in passion, the two lovers heard nothing and were blissfully unaware of the damage until they left a couple of hours later. Stunned, they stood at curbside, surveying the crumpled vehicle. The Packer quickly became enraged, threatening severe bodily harm to Stanley, since the singularity as well as the severity of the damage to the target left no doubt as to who the culprit was. Lily, her stomach churning sickeningly, tried to calm him down, knowing that as bad as things were, it would only get worse when she got home. What to do? They could call the cops, report a hit-and-run. No they couldn't, they realized. The extent of the damage made it plain it was no hit-and-run. Nor could the Packer go and beat the hell out of Stanley. In his vindictive mood, Stanley could easily deny ever doing anything, and file an assault charge on the Packer. And the player could not take the chance. It would get picked up off the police report and be in the local papers. Coach Lombardi, notoriously strait-laced, would not take kindly to this kind of publicity.

They decided Lily would drive the Packer home. The next morning early he called and made arrangements to have his car towed to a body shop where he got a loaner to drive. Lily went to her home and faced the music. She and Stanley had a knock-down, dragged out verbal battle, ending when Stanley demanded she move out. She agreed, as soon as she could. In the meantime, they spent the next couple of weeks living in the same house in an atmosphere very much like the border area between North and South Korea.

Ordinarily this wouldn't be all that extraordinary of a story. After all, countless marriages, including my own, have gone under because of identical circumstances. But two days after the Packer got his car back from the body shop in like-new condition, Stanley spotted it after bar time in the parking lot at the Pizza Hut. Stanley was not taking the failure of his marriage well. He had been drinking heavily since that fateful night when he discovered Lily's infidelity, and carried a heavy load of bitterness.

Now, once again drunk, perhaps emboldened by his success in getting away with his first demo-derby, he proceeded to once again ram the vehicle. Once more over and over, this time with greater vengeful speed, and in plain sight of the numerous customers inside the Hut.

Unfortunately in his drunken stupor, Stanley failed to recognize that, while closely matching the car of the man who placed the cuckold's horns on his head, it was, alas, not identical. Neither Lily nor the Packer player, nor their cars, were anywhere near the place. Attracted by the noise, people rose from their tables and rushed to the windows. Suddenly there was a shriek of disbelief.

"He's smashing my car! He's smashing my car!" a man yelled, his face frozen in stupefy disbelief. "Stop him! Christ! Who is that?!"

He dashed for the door but by now Stanley drove off, a dangling bumper on his front end dragging on the pavement. The man ran to the pay phone hanging on the wall and called the police. We stood by silently, looking at one another with helpless shrugs. Sometimes it's not only love that's blind. Sometimes it's vengeance.

The police arrested Stanley within minutes of his departure. He paid a heavy fine, had to make restitution, and only his unblemished past saved him from serving jail time.

He and Lily got divorced and in time her affair with the Packer ended. Months afterward she and I went out for a few drinks but by then I was over my crush on her and nothing ever developed between us. It was just as well. You never know when Stanley might have a relapse.

9

Poor Henry

One night when I was working service at the bar, one of the waitresses approached bearing a get-well card.

"Bob, we're taking up a collection for Clare. Her husband's really sick. He's in the hospital and they can't find out what's wrong with him."

Clare was one of the approximately twenty five women who worked as waitresses. I didn't know very much about her as she never came into the bar after her shift or on her nights off. She was middle-aged, a short, rather plain looking woman, and wore glasses with heavy black rims. She was quiet but did her job well, rarely making a mistake when she ordered drinks. I recalled that lately she'd seemed preoccupied, even solemn.

"That doesn't sound good, " I said, as I slipped a five into the envelope and signed the card.

"It's a mess. She's doing all she can. He's been there a couple of weeks already. He keeps getting weaker and weaker. She brings him soup and his favorite dishes from home because the hospital food so's crummy but he's not getting any better."

The card was circulated and, bolstered by especially generous contributions by Max and Fuzzy, over three hundred dollars was collected. Upon receiving it, it was reported, Clare broke down in tears of gratitude.

About a week later, I went back to the liquor storeroom to replace a bottle of Cointreau. Although we kept the bar stocked with back-up, it was mostly items that we sold a lot of. Some of the more exotic liquors would often last several months before we poured the last shot, so we'd simply not waste the space having a back-up for them. To get to the storeroom I had to pass through the break room. Clare was seated at the table, crying piteously, glasses pushed askew on her forehead.

"Poor Henry," she moaned. "He's just not getting any better. I don't know what to do." She burst into another round of sobbing. Around her a half a dozen waitress clustered, murmuring sympathy, handing her tissues, giving her comforting pats on the shoulder. I returned to the bar, feeling saddened at her pain and anguish.

The next evening Clare didn't come in to work or call. Fearing the worst, one of her co-workers tried calling her. When she didn't get an answer she called the hospital. It was suggested there that she call the police department. It was then that we found out Clare was in the Appleton jail, charged with murder.

As the doctors working on poor Henry became increasingly frustrated at his decline, they began to broaden their approach. One of them finally ordered a test for arsenic, something not typically done in the more normal course of events. Lo and behold, his system had a load of it. Reasonably certain that although the hospital food was lousy, it probably didn't contain arsenic, they asked themselves how he was getting it. Why, through all those tasty meals Clare had been giving him.

In the days that followed more news came to light. Poor Henry had a rather large life insurance policy taken out on him, a couple of hundred thousand, with his weeping wife as the beneficiary. And, as the police dug deeper, some years back Clare had been married before, and her husband had died with a rather vague cause of death listed on the death certificate. They had the body exhumed, and since arsenic evidently is a chemical that remains in body tissue, a subsequent autopsy showed that he'd also been poisoned. And, in what cliched the deal, Henry was recovering rapidly since he'd been placed on a regimen of only that lousy hospital food.

Clare pleaded guilty to multiple charges and got a lengthy sentence. Henry, after recovering, filed for divorce. I believe his wife missed her true calling. Based on what I saw that night in the break room she would have been a resounding success on stage. And I often wondered about Henry. After such an experience would a man ever get involved with a woman again? If so, I'd bet that they'd eat out in restaurants a lot.

10

Diamond Girl

In 1972 Dash Crofts and Jim Seals had a a huge top forty hit with their single, *Diamond Girl,* from their million selling album *Summer Breeze.* They continued their recording success for a decade, turning out hits and touring on the concert circuit, appearing before thousands of fans who paid anywhere from $20 to $40 for a ticket to hear them. But when they played at the Left Guard a year or so prior to their breaking into the Top Forty, almost no one had heard of them.

From the time it opened its doors, the Left Guard featured live music nightly. The bar room initially was small, compared to what would follow. Other than the bar, it had room for about a dozen tables lining two walls. In one corner was a small circular dance floor. Behind the dance floor Ron Larson stood, singing and playing his guitar through a small PA system. He played six mights a week, clad in a suit coat and tie, doing a credible job on covers such as "Both Sides Now," "If I Had A Hammer," "I Dig Rock and Roll Music," and similar tunes. Sometimes Fuzzy, Donny Anderson and a few other Packer players would get up and sing while Ron accompanied them. Sandy-haired, soft spoken, with a baby face, Ron also had a pilots license and a small plane, and sometimes he and Max would go off into the wild blue yonder. Once in the air, Ron would pass over the controls to Max, who had been a pilot in the Air Force.

As business increased, the Left Guard remodeled the bar room, gaining a fifty percent increase in floor space. The dance floor was made larger, tables added, and a low-level stage appeared in one corner. Ron was replaced by rock and roll bands. I think he was glad to go. You can only perform as a solo act six nights a week for so long before you begin to think you're trapped in the musical Twilight Zone. For a while various groups performed but eventually a band of local musicians established itself as the house band. Billed as the Glen Cass Trio, they consisted of Glen Cass on bass and vocals, Tom Vodapeck on drums and Rick Smith on guitar.

I got to know Glen and the other band members well, since a lot of the after-bar parties were made up of Packer players and their groupies, the band and their groupies, the Left Guard waitresses and bartenders, and an assortment of hardy clientele ready to jump in and pick off any strays. Glen and I, we discovered, had grown up five blocks apart in the Milwaukee suburb of West Allis, yet our paths had never crossed until Appleton. Although we ran with different groups in our callow youth, we still had some experiences in common, mostly based on the local residents who achieved fame among the neighborhood because of their goofy behavior. There was Ronnie Stader's dad, who worked in a iron foundry and on hot summer days would come home, talk off all his clothes and sit naked on his front porch, drinking cold beer. There was Kenny Lien's dad, who, while standing before our teen-age gaggle and putting a wad of tobacco in his cheek, announced that he "chewed Eight Brothers but spit seven sisters," an incredible non-sequiter that made no sense in spite of our knowing that Eight Brothers was the trade name of his tobacco. It sent us into gales of laughter. And Gilly Albert, who went on drunks so fierce that one of them culminated in his threatening his family and adjoining neighbors with a shotgun before retreating into his house. His family fled, the police arrived, barricaded off the street, and called for fire trucks to pull up in front of the house to provide cover. After a tense hour long stand-off, watched by the entire neighborhood, two policemen entered the house and found Gilly sound asleep at the kitchen table, the gun on the floor alongside him. He was awakened and dragged out to a squad car, his hands cuffed behind him. And there were the Spurls and the Mitchells, two hillbilly families from Tennessee who moved up to Milwaukee separately but somehow managed to buy houses with adjourning back yards in our neighborhood so they could continue a feud begun generations ago in the dark hollows of their native state. One of the Mitchell daughters, nick-named Popcorn, would be my very first puppy love and recipient of my first clumsy kisses. Later her brother Pete and I would run in the same gang of hoodlums on the streets of downtown West Allis.

In time the Glen Cass Trio regrouped. Rick Smith was replaced by Glen's brother Dan, who returned from working as a guitarist in California to become part of the band. He brought along a bass player who also joined the group, and Glen then switched to rhythm guitar.

The bass player who had arrived from California with Dan Cass was a very mellow guy. Joey X. was tall, quiet, good looking, married to a really sweet, pretty woman named Lana. Both he and his wife were practicing members of the Baha'i Faith, a monotheistic religion emphasizing the spiritual unity of mankind. I had some long conversations with them about their religion. They were quite willing to talk about it but did very little proselytizing, choosing, I think, to show its influence by example. They were both quiet, sincere, and genuinely liked people and expected the best from everyone.

Jim Seals and Dash Crofts were also members of the Baha'i Faith. They had been playing in various bands almost their entire lives, living in different areas of the country, before becoming a duo. They had met and become friends with Joey, Mary and Dan through the Baha'i network in California. They had just finished a gig in Canada and were on their way to Willamette, Illinois, where the oldest Baha'i House of Worship, and the only one in the United States, is located. Stopping in Appleton, they would jam with the band, and catch up on one another's lives while staying with Joey and Lana.

Jim Seals was small, lively, with intense dark eyes and a mustache and goatee, wearing a dockworkers hat and a leather jacket. An alto saxophone hung from his shoulder. Dash Crofts had the arch-typical hippie look, with long brown hair and a beard and mustache. They got up and played a long set backed by Glen and the others, giving an excellent performance, and the crowd loved them. Although not yet big-name recording artists, it was evident in their playing and vocal harmonies that they were poised for a breakthrough. Seals and Crofts only hung around for a few days before moving on. I got a chance to do a little visiting with them at a get-together at Joey and Lana's and later when they hit the big time, I was pleased for them, since they were really nice guys. Also, I now had another brush with greatness in addition to making pancakes for Linda Ronstadt. Added to my other experiences resulting from my working the bar at the Left Guard, I was getting a pretty good-size list.

Tom Vodapeck, the drummer with the band, and myself shared a different sort of bond. Over time we both dated and bedded the same willowy brunette, during separate relationships.

My relationship with her was a series of chaotic ups-and-downs that went on for over two years, periods of wild, passionate, alcohol-fueled nights both on the town and in the bedroom, with frequent fights and break-ups over alleged and real infidelities, finally culminating in her becoming pregnant. Frankly, I debated long and hard over whether to include this episode in this book. It's not something I recall with any pride or happiness and, actually, after all the years that have past, it still causes me pain. But I decided perhaps it would be good to include it, if only to show that not everything was all fun and games.

As I said, Debby and I had a tumultuous relationship. We went out together, lived together for a while, broke up and got back together several times. When we were together we spent a lot of our free time partying and drinking. Most of our fights and breakups involved one or the other of us stepping out and having sex with someone else. She had been taking birth control pills for quite a while but something went amiss. When we had been living together for the second time around she announced she was pregnant. We fought, an ugly, bitter fight of hurtful accusations, my demanding to know if she knew for sure that I was the father, why had she gone off the pill, she angry and bitter that I would ask such a thing, blame her when she'd faithfully taken her dosages, that I wouldn't take responsibility and marry her. She stormed out of the house, got into her car, and drove into our yard and, with a jarring crash, ran into the corner of the house.

I ran out of the house, horrified. She sat behind the wheel, fortunately unhurt, but crying bitterly, while the hood popped up and steam rose from the ruptured radiator. I got her inside and tried to calm her down. After she settled down somewhat I went back outside and pushed the hood down as best I could, backed the car up, and drove it a short ways up the driveway alongside the house. As I went back inside I paused to survey the damage to the house. It wasn't pretty but it looked like it was mostly cosmetic, damaged siding and some of the framing. It was an old wooden house and evidently well built. Wondering how in the hell I was going to explain this to the landlord, I went back inside and the two of us, emotionally spent, went to bed and slept without another word passing between us. The next day I got up and went to work. When I got home late that night, she had packed her things and was gone. So too her damaged car was gone from the driveway.

She moved back home into her parents house, who also lived in Appleton. While accepting her back in her condition with love, they were less than thrilled, as you can imagine. The sexual revolution had been going on for some time and unmarried mothers were no longer hurriedly swept off to some distant locale with a fraudulent excuse circulated to account for their absence. Still, illegitimate pregnancies were still seen as a social stigma. Debby, to give her all the credit in the world, handled it well. She continued to work and go about her daily life while carrying the baby to term. After she gave birth to a beautiful baby girl, she placed it for adoption.

Shamefully, I did not handle her pregnancy nearly as well. I chose to ignore it, and rebuffed her attempts to talk to me about it. I told myself I could not be sure I was the father, that it was an attempt to trick me into marriage, and other feeble excuses to salve my guilty conscience. Of course the facts of her pregnancy, including who the father was, swept rapidly among our friends and co-workers. While she was treated with kindness and sympathy by our friends and mutual acquaintances when she went out, I was treated like stepped-in dogshit. It didn't help that Debby, when we happened to be at the same party or gathering, would approach and offer me a plate of food, a drink, or sit quietly along side me, until I cracked under the pressure and bolted from the event like a snuff-chewing whore driven from a Methodist church. The result was there wasn't a woman in the entire city of Appleton that would be seen talking to me, let alone got out with me. Even my men friends, especially if they were married, tended to avoid me. In desperation, in time I began to drive to Oshkosh and Green Bay, to try and find a woman who would be seen with me.

Eventually, after she placed the baby for adoption, things settled down. Our lives went on and, when our paths would chance to cross, we got to where we could talk briefly, and be cordial to each other. As time passed, we met other love interests and entered into new relationships.

Four years went by. I had pretty much put the whole thing behind me when one night, the phone rang. The caller identified himself as James _____, a social worker from Sheboygan County, where my daughter had been born.

"My daughter?"

"Yes. Born to a Debby _____." He paused. "She named you as the father."

I stood silent, my mind hurriedly trying to sort out what he was telling me. What was he saying? Why was he calling now? Were they coming after me for child support? Why now? Why so long after?

"What's this about?" I finally blurted.

He told me. In order to understand, you have to know something about the times. Back then, when an unmarried woman found herself pregnant, her choices were limited. Although a few abortions clinics were operating openly, to many it was not an option due to how they viewed it. A woman who chose to keep the child and raise it herself generally found herself doing it totally on her own. If the alleged father would deny paternity, she would have to take him to court and face an ugly ordeal of questioning of her past sexual relationships prior to the pregnancy. In addition, blood tests were the only method available to determine paternity. And while an unlike blood type could rule out paternity, a like type was not accepted as conclusive proof. Faced with this, as well as the social stigma for herself and the child, the lack of jobs available for women that provided a decent income and other obstacles, the majority of women would go away somewhere, have the baby and place it for adoption. And while a father would be named when filling out the paper work for the adoption, it was assumed by his indifference to the birth that he had no interest in its resolution. It was considered the mother's signature was enough.

This all changed due to a horrific case that took place, ironically enough, in Wisconsin. A boy born to an unwed mother had been adopted by parents who gave him a loving and stable home. Now, at the age of five, his biological father, who lived in Florida, had come forth and demanded custody. The father was a less than savory individual and everyone connected with the case felt it would definitely be a poor development to place the boy with him. However, the father had never signed off on his parental rights. After a fierce legal battle, the judge had no choice but to turn the boy over to his father.

Within a year the boy died of child abuse at the hands of his biological father. The story received a lot of publicity and people everywhere were outraged. But the judge's hands had been tied. The rights of biological parents are viewed as superior to any other claims, or so it was ruled, in spite of the tragic outcome of this particular case. The ruling, and the inadvertent neglect to have biological fathers sign off their rights at the time of adoption, prompted a massive effort on the part of adoption agencies everywhere to rectify this oversight. They would go back and contact as many men as they could locate and ask them to sign away any parental rights. And this is why I was being called. My daughter had been adopted shortly after her birth without my consent. Would I now give up my rights to her?

Was she in a good home,? I asked.

He assured me she was. I agreed to sign and relief was evident in his voice as he thanked me. I realized just how important this was to the agency when he also offered to come to my house the next evening with the papers.

He arrived and of course there were half a dozen pages packed with fine print. I hesitated, not because I was reluctant to give up my rights, but because you are always warned about "the fine print." But I decided to hell with it, if this was a trick someone had gone to a lot of trouble to set it up. I signed.

We chatted a bit as he put the papers into his briefcase. He said he'd checked the agency records and the child was doing fine. When she was older she'd have to be told about her being a carrier but otherwise she was fine.

A what?

He bit his lip, chagrined. He'd evidently assumed I knew something and now he had perhaps gone too far. But, since legally I had now given up any rights, he evidently felt ok with telling me.

Debby had an older sister but no brothers. Her sister was married and had given birth to a boy and a girl. Of course I already knew this. What I didn't know was that after Debby had given birth to her daughter, her nephew had developed muscular dystrophy. With muscular dystrophy many times males get the disease while the women do not. But they are the carriers. Subsequent tests showed while her niece would not get the disease, she was a carrier. Any male children she gave birth to would develop the disease. Based on this, Debby had been tested and it was found that she too carried this gene. So too did the child she placed for adoption. Her adoptive parents had been made aware of this and in time, when the daughter reached child-bearing age, she would be told.

He left and I sat in my darkened house, thinking for a long time. I'm going to end this chapter now, Diamond Girl. Like I said, it wasn't all fun and games. Sometimes there were huge regrets.

11

1000 Yard Club Banquets*

*Be warned, the following account is how I remember it.

One of the premier events of the time began at the Left Guard. There are a couple of differing stories as to how it got started. In one version, the National 1000 Yard Club banquet started when one year in the early nineteen sixties a banquet was held to honor Red Smith. Smith, a legendary sports writer with with the New York Herald Tribune, had grown up in Green Bay, and was an avid Packer fan. The banquet was a success, well attended by Packer players and local dignitaries and their wives and girlfriends. When it was proposed for the following year, Smith modestly pointed out that while it was a nice gesture, he didn't feel comfortable with all the hoopla and accolades on an annual basis. Someone then came up with the idea of honoring the NFL running backs who had gained over a thousand yards rushing in a single, regular season. Any money raised over and above the costs of the event would be given to a charity.

Currently, there is an annual event called the Red Smith Sports Award banquet hosted in the Appleton area. It's been going on since 1965. But it's not the same Red Smith as the sports writer. It's named after a Appleton native who played professional baseball and football. This Red Smith also played for the Green Bay Packers in 1927, and in 1929 as a line coach under Curly Lambeau. Formally organized in 1965 by local businessmen, it is a non-profit organization that hosts an awards banquet which honers athletes and other sports figures in numerous sports. It uses the money it raises to provide student athlete scholarships for recipients in northeastern Wisconsin.

This is virtually identical to the National 1000 Yard Club when it existed, both in the way it was organized and its purpose. Also, both organizations were founded within a year of each other. But to determine if one spawned the idea for the other, it is impossible to say. The fact that both the sports writer and the former Packer had the same name as well as local ties also could have led to some confusion as to the above story.

There is another, more straight forward and better documented version of how it began. Former Packer player Tony Canadeo, who in 1949 became the third running back in the NFL to gain 1,000 yards, still lived in Green Bay. He approached Fuzzy, Max and their partner in the Left Guards, a restauranteur named Bill Martine, and suggested an event to honor NFL running backs who had gained over a thousand yards in a single, regular season.

Prior to 1961 the NFL had a twelve game regular season. In 1961 it went to fourteen games. The season length, typical running back size, as well as team strategies and defenses, made gaining a thousand yards on the ground a singular achievement. The idea was well received, and the partners went to work. Along with Mal Kennedy, who later became executive director of the NFLPA, they convinced over 100 local businesses to pitch in $100 apiece to cover costs and become founding members.

In 1964 the first banquet was held in the Neenah-Menasha Elks Club, honoring the 11 running backs who had gained 1000 yards in the seasons prior to that year. The Elks Club was chosen as the site because the Left Guard in Menasha was too small, and the Appleton location had yet to be built. The event included a golf outing for the players and a parade through downtown Menasha. As the event grew in size and popularity, it was held at various locations in the area. Regardless of where the actual banquet took place, the Left Guards in Appleton and Menasha became established as the de facto centers of the action.

As might be expected, the 1000 Yard Club banquets were extraordinary events. Once a year in June, the Fox River Valley became the center of the football universe. In addition to the honorees, the Left Guard would be packed to capacity with football players from every team in the league, Hollywood actors, local CEO's and politicians, and all the men and women who came to gawk at them. Or, for the common folk, perhaps have a brush with greatness by actually speaking to one of them. And for the really lucky guys, to swoop down on a sexy female groupie who, since she was part of a gaggle that greatly outnumbered the available glitterati, might be willing to settle for someone less.

The party started during the week prior to the actual Saturday night banquet as the attendees came into town. As bartenders, we loved working those nights. The tips were fantastic, and there were the bragging rights. ".......when I was talking to Paul Hornung when he was here for the 1000 Yard Club banquet...." was a good way to get a woman's attention at a house party in the weeks to follow. In reality however the bar would be jammed and we would be pretty much busting our asses making drinks the entire night, with little time for conversation. Still, there were those moments.

"My God, he's beautiful," one of the local girls breathed, when she saw OJ Simpson live for the first time as he entered the bar. Dressed in white slacks and shirt, accompanied by his first wife, he was strikingly handsome as he gracefully made his way through the crowd.

Don Meredith, the Dallas Cowboys quarter back, was also there. When the band took a break, he grabbed a guitar, stepped up to the mike, and did a solo rendition of the Janis Joplin song, "Oh Lord, Won't you Buy Me," and he did it well.

Hollywood was represented by Gardner McKay, Phil Crosby and Robert Lansing sitting at the bar. A couple of out-of-town professional ladies also made an appearance. However, they didn't stay more than one night. "Honey, there's too many amateurs here for a working girl to compete," one of them told me as they gathered up their purses and left.

Over the years it hosted a stunning array of football players, past and present.

Y.A. Tittle was there. George Blanda. Rocky Blier, who had grown up in Appleton. Franco Harris. Larry Kelly. Jim Brown. Stu Voight. Jimmy Carter, who had inherited the tough job of replacing Ray Nitsche at middle linebacker for the Packers. Bart Starr. Jerry Kramer. Ken Bowman. Donny Anderson. Herb Adderly. Doug Hart. Willie Davis. Willie Wood. Fran Tarkenton. Gayle Sayers. Of course Fuzzy, Max, Paul Hornung, Ray Nitzche, and numerous other past and present Packers. In 1968 Vince Lombardi addressed the attendees after dinner. In 1970 it was Weeb Eubank. Another year Pete Rozelle spoke. Other coaches who attended included Don Shula, George Allen and Al Davis. Sports announcers Howard Cosell and Chris Schenkel also came.

By the time it ended in 1977, it had honored 41 NFL running backs, starting with Beatie Feathers in 1934. In 1965 an award was added to honor the outstanding blocker of the year and 13 NFL linemen received the annual award.

In 1966 Dick Bass, the Los Angeles Rams running back, was an honoree. He started his acceptance speech with a joke that I enjoyed and still tell to this day.

A blind man is at a bus stop. His seeing eye dog raises his snout and bites him in the leg. The blind man reaches into his pocket and gives the dog a piece of dog candy. Another man standing there is incredulous.

"Excuse me, sir," he says to the blind man. "I know it's none of my business. But your seeing eye dog just bit you in the leg and you rewarded him with a treat?"

"Treat, no way," the blind man replies. "I'm just finding out where his head is so I can kick his ass!" It got a big laugh.

While Dick Bass was comfortable addressing the large audience, not so with some of the other honorees. As bartenders, we had the opportunity to see what went on behind the scenes. It gave some of us mere normal mortals a perverse pleasure in seeing some of the most feared, hulking, physically intimidating football players in the National Football League cut down to size by stage fright. Sweating profusely, legs trembling, muttering their prepared remarks over and over, they waited off stage, hidden from the guests, to get up to the podium and get it over with.

Beatie Feathers was at several of the 1000 Yard Club banquets. At first glance it seemed odd that he was there, let alone being greeted with such acclaim by the other players. He was, especially when standing next to any of them, small in stature, and by now a wizened, balding old man. However, he had a lively, gregarious manner so I first assumed he was one of those persons who ingrain themselves with the rich and famous primarily because of their eccentricities. However, I learned later he richly deserved to be in their company. In 1934, while playing with the Chicago Bears, he was the first professional football player to gain 1000 yards rushing. Even then, at 5'10" and 185 pounds, he was small to be playing professional football, let alone gain 1000 yards. But evidently he was tough and extremely fast, able to run under and around the bigger players much in the manner of the NBA's Spud Webb.

Beatie also had a code of honor. One of the ladies who came into the Guard on a regular basis was Leah C. Leah was in her twenties, very attractive, with blonde, almost white hair that she wore in a style much like Tina Turner's. She favored white--white dresses and white, calf high boots. She laughed a great deal, flirted easily, drank moderately, and, although she liked to have a good time, was discreet in the number and types of men she left with. Altogether a fine lady.

On the Friday night prior to the dinner, she was at The Guard. Despite the frantic work pace and the large crowd, we managed to exchange smiles and a few words. About ten o'clock that evening I looked up from bartending to see two ambulance attendants wheeling a stretcher down the hall past the bar into the banquet room in back. Leah had broken her leg, the word spread quickly. She was running away from Jim Carter when it happened. Running away, like he was chasing her?? Well, it was more kind of like they were goofing around. However, Beatie, who saw only the chasing part, felt it wasn't proper for a man the size of Jim Carter to force his attentions on such a lovely damsel as Leah. As she was being placed on the stretcher, Beatie accosted Jim and an argument broke out. After some angry words and a couple of shoves, cooler heads prevailed, stepped between the two men, and restored order.

Some months later, I had an opportunity to get to know Leah better. And Sandy, her dog. Although we'd always been friendly over a long time, somehow we'd never gone beyond that. Then one night I sat down next to her when my shift was over and things moved in a new direction. A couple of hours later I was following her to her second story apartment, above a store that sold sewing fabrics. As we ascended her stairs, a verse from a Lou Rawls song popular at the time hummed pleasantly in my alcohol-addled brain.

"...When I was 21, it was a very good year, a very good year for big city girls, who lived up the stairs, with all their perfume hair, and it came undone, when I was 21...."

I was definitely looking forward to seeing Leah's hair, along with her dress and other items of clothing, being undone.

As we reached the top she paused outside the door.

"You'll have to wait a minute. My dog Sandy's a girl.

And she doesn't like men.

I'll go inside and hold her and then you come in and I'll introduce you. Then it'll be ok."

Whatever. A moment later she called and I entered. Sandy, a good-sized mutt of indeterminate breed, eyed me balefully as Leah held her by the collar. Her fur was pure white and she did resemble Little Orphan Annie's dog of the same name. "It's ok," Leah reassured Sandy. "He's a friend. It's ok."

I gave Sandy a tentative pat on the head. Leah released her and she gave me a sniff, then padded to her doggy bed, nails clicking on the hardwood floor, where she flopped down and licked her chops. I followed Leah into her bedroom.

The remainder of the evening was extremely pleasant. Leah was skillful, sweet, and passionate. I responded in kind and we spent a couple of very pleasurable hours. We fell asleep in each others arms, the perfect Hollywood scenario. The next morning I awoke and looked over. Leah was still peacefully asleep. Good. I could slip away without the whole morning-after awkwardness of making excuses for leaving. I stuck a leg out of the covers and began to slip out of bed.

"Grrrrrrrr."

I looked down. Sandy lay on the floor next to my side of the bed, licking her chops at me expectantly. Hastily I pulled my leg back under the covers. What the hell. I thought we were friends. I looked around for my clothes. They lay crumpled on the floor. Sandy rose, and as if reading my mind, walked over and flopped down on top of them. Shit. Some minutes went by and then my bladder began to nudge at me. Oh great. Now I had to piss. I stuck my foot out again.

"Grrrrrrrr." A little louder. Shit. This was getting serious. I glanced over at Leah who was still asleep. However, I could swear she had a tiny smile on her face. Maybe a pleasant dream? I tried a third and final time. This time Sandy stood up and opened her mouth, showing me her bright, sharp shiny teeth as she grrrred. I gave up and woke up Leah.

"Good morning." She smiled happily as she sat up and stretched.

"I need to use the bathroom."

"It's there," she pointed.

"I know. But when I try and get out of bed Sandy growls at me."

"Oh she won't hurt you."

Yeah. Maybe. Maybe not. However, the idea of getting up and standing along side the bed totally naked while a female dog that doesn't like men is crouched there ready to strike held little appeal for me. Still, to remain motionless would appear cowardly. I got an idea.

"How about some coffee?" I asked.

"Sure." She got out of bed and slipped into a robe and headed for the kitchen. As I'd hoped, Sandy padded after her. I jumped out of bed and scampered to the bathroom, returning a moment later to dress.

After some coffee and toast, a bit of morning small talk in her cheerful, sunlit kitchen, and my getting her phone number, she walked me to the door. We kissed good by.

"I'll call you," I lied.

She smiled. I looked down at her dog. "Good by, Sandy."

"Grrrrrrrrr," Sandy replied. She must have known I was lying. Good luck, Jim Carter.

12

The Horsefeather, Freight Train Danny, Rubber Teat Cups
and a Lawn Jockey

My bartending career in Appleton was not exclusive to
the Left Guard. One of the other establishments I worked
at was The Horsefeather, a bar that featured nude dancing.
Located outside of the Appleton city limits in the Town of
Menasha, it was able to take advantage of the Town's lack
of ordinances at the time restricting nudity in bars.

The building had previously been a supper club with a
dismal past, having opened and closed in rapid succession
under several previous owners. It was located on Doty
Island, which was not a true island, but rather a section of
high ground in the Fox River, separated from the west
shore by an area of swamp. To reach the old, somewhat
rundown building, you drove down a long, bumpy gravel
road that passed over a set of railroad tracks. The current
operator who was leasing the buildings was a Telly Savalas
look-a-like named BJ Eddy. He appeared in the area out of
nowhere and never volunteered any information to anyone
about his past.

After opening up the place and, after two months
passed of barely serving enough customers to keep the

lights on, BJ realized he needed a different path to success. He fired his waitresses, hired a new staff of young, good-looking women, and had them go topless as they served the burgers and fries. Since this was still an era where public nudity was largely confined to sleazy strip clubs in large cities, the novelty of this new style of dining spread like wildfire. Business boomed. Taken by surprise, the Town Board began to wrestle with how to deal with this issue. BJ promptly hired a lawyer to fight a delaying action. He also realized that his customers could care less about burgers so he quickly eliminated the food operation, did some remodeling, and became what today is euphemistically referred to as a "gentleman's club."

BJ's tenure lasted about 3 years. Although he was able to keep the Town at bay over the nudity issue by various legal maneuverings for a time, they began to come at him in other ways. Various fire and building inspectors showed up, and would cite the operation with a long list of violations. State tax agents also began to call, checking to make sure all the booze had tax stamps and the bills were paid, and looking for time keeping and employment violations. Local undercover police would drop in to check for under-age drinking or anything else they could ticket for.

BJ dealt with it all by giving a text book lesson in how to run a con, showing an innate sense of when to close shop and leave town that could only have come from running various scams in the past. He began to pay only enough to get by, dribbling out money to suppliers only when they threatened to stop deliveries. And he gave priority only to those issues that could directly shut down his business. For the last couple of months of his operation, he quit paying his bills altogether. Unlike peas and potatoes, liquor is taxed heavily by the state government and liquor bills owed to the suppliers had to be paid within 30 days of delivery. If they continued to sell you product when your account was past due, they could get in serious trouble themselves with the state department of revenue, in addition to the tavern owner. So when they cut off deliveries BJ began the strictly illegal practice of buying booze from a liquor store operator and re-selling it at the bar.

The wheels of justice turn slowly but turn they do. One day when I showed up for work the front door was secured with a shining massive padlock and hasp. A state department of revenue notice was posted above it. The Horsefeather was closed due to unpaid taxes. I wasn't surprised. The rumors had been flying and I'd seen enough of BJ's antics to know the end was near. However, he had always made sure I was paid on time so I bore no ill-will towards the man. Not so the legal authorities. They wanted his blood so bad they could taste it.

But, much to their dismay, BJ was nowhere to be found, having left town the night before with a long-legged red-headed dancer named Connie and a suitcase full of money. In a nice parting touch, after he left, the various state and county prosecutors found that he had put the entire operation in his wife's name when he began. A small, diminutive woman with the IQ of a turnip, she had been seen so seldom around the place most of us didn't know BJ was even married. She was totally ignorant of what had been going on and, after interviewing her, the state and local prosecutors disgustedly gave up any hope of prosecution and instead had to settle for the satisfaction of knowing they had closed down this hotbed of sinful, lewd nakedness.

Right up to the end, my working at the Horsefeather was one hell of an interesting time. The dancers worked afternoon matinees and evenings five times a week.

I was in my twenties and after about a month of starting to bar tend there, I was somewhat shocked to realize I could actually become bored with naked women. I learned later that there is actually a therapeutic technique based on the idea of constantly exposing someone to what they are adverse to, and eventually they become de-sensitized to it. Well, I'm definitely not adverse to naked women but the constant presence of nakedness did lead to, if not desensitization, a somewhat jaded outlook. And at the Horsefeather, believe me, it was constant. Every time you looked around, there were bare tits and ass jiggling. Different sizes, shapes, colors, all times of day and night, bare fronts, rears, sides, backs, sometimes on a level of intimacy normally only found in a doctor's office.

For example, during the matinee, the dancers would

eschew the stage and get up on the bar top, clad only in high heels and make-up. They would make their way down the bar, jukebox blaring, crouching down and spreading their legs just inches from the customers noses. It certainly broadened the definition of what constituted dancing. One of the ladies in particular enhanced the eroticism by taking off the eye glasses worn by various customers and rubbing them in her crotch, and then slipping them back on their noses. Dazed by the whole experience, they would sit shell-shocked, and their opaque lenses coated with vaginal juices would remind me of those black-and-white sketches of blind beggars in a Victorian novel—you know, the ones where they omit the eyes.

Most of the dancers, to put it bluntly, were bat-shit crazy. Some of them were on drugs—mostly amphetamines, which at the time were freely available as prescription diet pills. Talking to them was like having a conversation with a pinball machine. Many of them were in denial about their actual occupation--dancing naked in front of large groups of leering men—having convinced themselves that what they were doing was "performance art". Some of them would be accompanied by a boy friend, who generally was a greasy looking biker-type or some pseudo-tough guy who would refer to his girl friend as "the old lady,' or "the bitch." Generally he would spend his time drinking at the bar, running up a substantial bar tab which BJ would deduct from the dancer's wages before he paid her. While sitting there he cloaked himself in a proprietary, macho attitude towards everyone and everything, especially his "woman", while dropping dark hints about his shady life of crime and mayhem. Mostly these guys were full of bullshit, sad, posturing social misfits as deluded about their lives as their girlfriends. Their stories were invariably boring as hell.

Occasionally one of the dancers would show up and be fairly normal, or as normal as you can possibly be when you're making your living taking all your clothes off in public three times an evening. Stacy was one such lady. During our conversations, she showed a firm grasp on reality, talking about how she was saving her money, planning on using it to pay for college.

"I'm good with numbers. I'm going to get a degree in finance," she explained. "I've got a good head on my shoulders."

I didn't doubt it for a second. When not on stage, she drank little, and when finished with her act would go to the dressing room instead of hanging around the bar. She was dead-set against drug use, and spoke disparagingly about other dancers who would free-lance prostitute, or use their sexuality to entice cash and other favors from some of the more gullible customers.

"I'm saving it for the guy who puts a ring on my finger," she declared.

On that point I must have looked skeptical.

"Look," she explained. "I know what you're thinking. But

hey, I'm nice looking, got a great body. Why shouldn't I use it to make money? Is it any different than some guy with speed and brawn using his attributes to make money playing football?"

I guess not, I told her. If you can overlook the fact that by the time your act ends you're on stage in front of a roomful of horny men, who are mentally screwing you. And all your wearing is a black top hat, a white bow-tie and black fuck-me stiletto heels, and carrying a cane. This was Stacy's finale, by the way. When she first stepped out she'd be wearing a black tuxedo outfit that had been modified so its pieces could be easily shed as she danced. One of her more popular moves, after she'd gotten rid of her tuxedo, was to take take off the top hat and push her ample breasts into it, where it jauntily bounced as she pushed out her chest and shimmied. What she did with the cane I'll leave to your imagination.

"That's exactly my point," she countered triumphantly. "I can do all that but that's all. I don't fuck anybody, I don't do a bunch of bad shit. I respect myself."

Compared to the others, she was a refreshing change. When she left I was sad to see her go and wished her a lot of luck.

Not so with one of the other ladies, whose gimmick was snake dancing. Her name was Esmeralda or some such, and she would come up from downstairs to do her act with one or sometimes two long snakes draped around her body. I don't know if they were boas or pythons or anacondas or what, but I knew I hated them. Their names were Sammy and Sally, and of course the first time she came upstairs from the basement dressing room, she came behind the bar so we could meet them. Todd, my bartender partner, was ok with it and actually petted them. Me, I was pressed up against the back bar as far away as possible. So naturally Esmeralda did what people always do when your scared shitless of a creature, they bring it to you.

"They won't hurt you," she purred, extending one of their heads to me. "They like people. Here, just pet Sally."

By this time I was scrunched half-way up the back bar trying to escape, my face white with fear. Todd was laughing hysterically. Even the customers were laughing. "Later," I croaked.

For the next two weeks I lived in hell. The word spread of my terror and the other bartenders thought it hysterically funny to wait until I wasn't looking, then throw a knotted bar towel to hit my legs, shout "Snake!" and watch me jump three feet in the air. The ice machine was located in the basement. To get to it you had to pass by the dressing room for the dancers. In the past, I was always eager to go for ice, since it afforded a chance to chat with the dancers who often left the door open. Clad in a robe or wrap or less, they would be re-doing make-up or reading a magazine until it was time for their performance. Somehow being partially dressed made them that much more enticing. When Esmeralda arrived, however, she kept her dancing partners in a box in the dressing room. I immediately lost all enthusiasm for fetching ice. But sometimes if I was working alone, I had no choice. I would race down the stairs, jam the ice bucket full while spilling ice cubes all over the place, and charge back up to safety, all the while keeping my eyes glued to the snake box in the dressing room. She also took it upon herself to convince me my reptilian phobia was unfounded and would often come behind the bar both before and after her act, snakes dangling between her boobs, and talk to me. Nothing, however, could change the way I felt. But her act was very popular, and BJ was talking about holding her over for another week since business was so good. I shuddered at the thought.

Then one day she came upstairs, sobbing hysterically. "I can't find Sammy," she gulped frantically. "He's not in his box."

Oh, just fuckin great. Now the Horsefeather was a good-sized old wood structure, who'd had lots of previous tenants running food and bar operations. The basement alone was enormous, dark, damp, and piled to the ceiling with old fixtures and equipment of indeterminate age and origin left behind by defunct operators. Now we had a six foot python crawling about its innards, ready to pop out anywhere and, most likely, right in my face. A search ensued, conducted by everyone working at the time except yours truly. After all, someone had to tend bar.

No trace of Sammy was ever found. Esmeralda was

inconsolable. She moped around as if her best lover had died. Sally, Sammy's mate, seemed to pick up on her mistress's mood, and Sammy's physical absence as well, and became limp to the point where the customers began to ask "Is that fuckin snake hanging on her real?" When her stint ended BJ chose not to renew her contract. When she left she gave us a phone number where we could call if Sammy ever showed up. Fat chance.

After she was gone a rumor started that I had actually murdered Sammy. I defended my innocence by explaining that it was impossible, since, in order to do the deed, I would have had to get much closer to Sammy then was physically possible for me. All I know, is that for the remainder of my time working there, I absolutely dreaded going to the basement. I was sure Sammy was hanging among the floor joists above me, poised to drop down and strangle me.

Another scenario is possible. After wintering over in the basement, Sammy may have slithered out and taken up residency in the marshy area surrounding Doty Island. After mating with some native snake species, his offspring arrived and thrived on the pollutants dumped into the Fox River by the paper mills. By now the clan has evolved into a nest of giant monster reticulating snakes. On a warm summer evening a boatload of unsuspecting teen age boys and their bikini-clad hottie girlfriends come ashore to party. The music booms out into the night, the Red Bull and Jaegermiester flow, the campfire blazes along with the testosterone-fueled urges of the sex-crazed teen-agers. Just as the orgy is about to begin, Sammy's offspring strike. The nubile young bodies of the girls are wrapped in the hideous, slimy coils of the monster snakes, while the boys are strangled and devoured as they try to defend them. Note to self: Contact Hollywood as soon as possible about movie treatment guidelines.

One Monday night, Danny L. stopped in to the Horsefeather. I had worked with Dan at the Left Guard, and he was still employed there as a full-time bartender. A chunky, good-natured guy with dark, curly hair, he was an excellent bartender and we got along well. I was glad to see him.

There is, among those in the food and beverage business, a spirit of esprit de corp, a bond developed by the shared and unique experience of waiting on the public when they've been consuming alcohol. It's bolstered by the craziness that develops in the late evening hours, the after bar parties, the notoriety attached to the profession, and the impact of working most nights when everyone else is out having fun. Also, Appleton at this time was a small enough city to host no more than about a dozen supper clubs and go-to bars. With this limited number of establishments, no matter which one you worked at, you eventually would get to know anyone else working in the trade. This wove our bond even tighter. Most of the clubs closed on Mondays or Tuesdays, since they were the

129

slowest business days of the week. These, then, were our nights off, when we'd go out and get the attention and service that we worked hard on other nights to provide to others.

Professional courtesy dictated that, if you were working behind the bar, you never charged another bartender or waitress for his or her drink when they stopped in your place. If they insisted, or offered to buy a round for themselves and their group, you might take their money. But only rarely. On the other hand, if you were the recipient of this courtesy, you tipped often and generously.

Monday and Tuesday nights the Horsefeather did not have dancers, so they were typically slow nights. This particular night, In addition to Danny, some other people in the trade stopped by and hung around, playing the jukebox, shaking dice, drinking and talking. It was an easy, relaxed time. Unlike most nights of racing around waiting on demanding and drunken customers, this one was more like hosting a quiet house party. Bar time neared, the place cleared out, with Danny the last to leave. I scooped up my tips, cleaned up the glasses and re-stocked the coolers, put away the till drawer, turned off the lights and left, locking the door behind me. I hadn't gone too far up the gravel road leading from the Horsefeather to Highway 41 when Danny appeared in my headlights, trudging towards me.

"Danny, what's up?" I asked when I pulled over and he opened the door.

"Shit. I smashed up my front end. Can you give me a ride home?"

He got in and a minute later we passed his Cadillac, sitting crookedly by the side of the road, its left front corner just inches from the gravel roadway, the tire and rim a mangled mess. "I took the damn tracks too fast," he explained.

I knew exactly what he meant. We had just driven over a set of railroad tracks and, where they crossed, the road rose in a steep, short climb. On a heavily traveled road, this dangerous condition would have been remedied long ago. But since our road dead-ended at the club, and in the past had gotten little use, the Town had simply put up a couple of warning signs and let it go at that. If you traveled the road frequently, you would remember to slow down before the tracks. But Danny, who had visited the bar for his first time that night, had taken the incline too fast. The front end of the Cadillac had smashed down, rendering it unfit to drive. With the lateness of the hour both the cost of getting a wrecker to tow the car and the fact that Danny, while not drunk, had been drinking, made it prudent to wait until morning to deal with his wrecked car. I dropped him at his apartment where he said his girlfriend would give him a ride to work tomorrow, and he'd call a repair shop to pick up his car.

He never got the chance. About 9 am a heavy knocking at his door woke him.

He groggily opened it to find two burly policemen standing there, and they promptly arrested him for wrecking a train. It seems that when the front end of the Cadillac had smashed into the roadway, it had knocked one of the railroad tracks loose. Early that morning a string of Soo Line freight cars being pushed by a locomotive came chugging up the tracks, hit the damaged rail and several cars tipped over. Fortunately no one was injured but the railroad people were understandably upset. They saw the damaged Cadillac, the ruptured rail, and put the two together.

The cops took Danny to the police station and raised some serious hell over the whole thing. They grilled Danny, saying should have reported the accident when it happened, that he had left the scene, and, since he was departing from the Horsefeather, he must have been drunk. By this time he was definitely awake and alert, and wisely demanded an attorney. He also called his girlfriend who then called me to fill me in. When they asked him how he got home, he was quick-witted enough to say he'd hitchhiked. So the next day, when a detective dropped by my place, I had my story together. Yes, Danny had been in the bar. I didn't remember when he left, he'd been there a couple of hours but only had three of four beers. I guess I must have seen the damaged car by the side of the road but didn't think much of it. No, I didn't see him along the road. The detective wrote it all down, eyed me skeptically, and left.

In the end it worked out pretty well. Danny got a ticket

and a good-sized fine but, considering the extent of the damage, it could have been a lot worse. He also got the sobriquet of Freight Train Dan and the unique distinction of being the only bartender that we knew of who had single-highhandedly wrecked a train. We held this feat in high regard.

Frank S---- and his son Ross owned and operated a supper club called, not surprisingly, S----'s. It was one of the old, established eating places in Appleton but, much like Schlitz beer, at the time its clientele was dwindling due to death and age. The impact of both Nino's and the Left Guard opening up also had a negative effect on their business.

At the time, myself, Chuck D. and his brother Jim were all working at the Left Guard. We also were renting a three bedroom house in Neenah. For us, and other both married and single bartenders, our typical work day went something like this. Sleep until 11 am or noon, get up, shower and shave, and head over to S----'s. There we would grab a sandwich and gather at the bar, shaking dice and gossiping until four o'clock or so when we'd head to our different establishments to start our night shift. We liked S----'s, since we pretty much had the place to ourselves through the daytime. Evening business there wasn't much better.

The dice game of choice was called Ship, Captain and Crew, a game still very popular today. It involved shaking five dice in the leather dice cup (today made out of rubber) and either spilling them or slamming the cup down, to empty it on the bar. You needed to roll a six—your "captain"-- a five, your "ship," and a four—your "crew,"

before the remaining two die were added up to get your point total. You could not get points until you rolled your ship, captain and crew, in the correct order. You got three shakes and could set aside any of the dice that met the above criteria. If you got your ship, captain and crew and points in less than three shakes, the other players either had to tie or beat your point total in the same number of shakes. 12 points, the two sixes—called boxcars—along with a six, five and four rolled in one flop was the best shake possible. We usually played for dollar per player pots, anteing another dollar to the existing pot when a game was tied, and paying an additional dollar to any winner that rolled boxcars. Sometimes we'd raise the beginning ante to five dollars and in a single afternoon you could easily win or lose sixty to one hundred dollars, a goodly sum in those days.

Later on, after a career change, I worked for an engineering firm in Madison, Wisconsin. One of our clients was a company called Hi-Life Rubber Company located in Johnson Creek, Wisconsin. We were involved in the planning and design of an addition to their manufacturing facility. The company, owned and operated by a affable man and his three sons, made a single product, rubber teat cups. These are the inflatable rubber inserts placed inside the four metal cylinders that dangle from the top of a milking machine. When the machine is connected to a compressed air line, its mechanism squirts a quick burst of air into each cylinder, exerting pressure on the rubber insert and then releasing it, thus mimicking the squeezing action of the human hand on the cow's teat. The cow releases its milk which is stored in the milk machine and emptied by hand or sent directly through a line to a cooling tank.

Hi-Life Rubber produced an enormous number of these teat cups every year. The machinery that extruded the rubber into the correct shape and thickness was produced in Germany and very expensive. Hence they had little competition. Also, the cups had to be both soft and flexible, which meant that after a certain number of uses, they wore out and had to be replaced. Since dairy cows needed to be milked twice a day regardless whether the economy was good or bad, the business was pretty much, as the brothers would say with a grin, "inflation-proof."

While most of the factory addition would be used to expand the teat cup line, one of the sons had convinced the others of the need to diversify the product line. In the new addition, the family was installing a couple of new machines that would produce dice cups made of rubber. These cups, unlike the leather ones, would rarely wear out, no matter how hard they were abused. Within a few years they took over the market, and the leather cups became a thing of the past. Hi-Life Rubber continued its success with their development of a small but diversified product line--

teat cups and dice cups.

Ross S----, Frank's son, would manage the day shift at their restaurant and since business was slow, he would often bar tend as well. One day, when our group was at the bar shaking dice, Ross lamented how their business was not so good. He wondered why none of the Packer players stopped in and hung around his place, and maybe we could mention it to some of them since it would bolster his business. Ross was a nice enough guy but, although he had graduated from Notre Dame University and wasn't overtly stupid, we had figured out some time ago he lacked street smarts. In short, he was somewhat easy to fool. Chuck took this opportunity to mess with him.

"Well you know Ross, the reason they won't come in is they're offended by that lawn jockey outside your front entrance."

Ross was baffled. "What do you mean?"

By this time the civil rights movement had been well underway, but the struggle still continued in various parts of the country in ways of shameful ugliness, and the strife often aired on the nightly news. However, in the Fox River Valley, blacks, while few in number, if not always welcomed with open arms, were generally accepted. Unlike when I worked in Milwaukee, I had yet to see any blatant prejudice exhibited in the area. This was due in a large part to Vince Lombardi, who, on becoming coach of the Packers, had spread the word among the business community that any place that did not welcome the black players in their establishment would not see any of the white players in their place either. Certainly any Packer players, white or black, would have been welcome at S----'s, as both Ross and his father were huge Packer fans.

But S----'s had been built and furnished a long time ago and had changed very little. As you walked to the front door, on the porch you passed one of those porcelain caricatures of a grinning black boy with gleaming white teeth, clad in red and white jockey apparel and holding a lantern in one hand. Back then, while not common, they were not that unusual. However, Chuck, who was among us our white, liberal, out-spoken proponent of civil rights and vehemently anti-war, had mentioned a couple of times that he found the statue offensive. But none of the black Packer players who frequented the Left Guard had ever mentioned it and frankly I doubt any of them even knew it existed, since they didn't patronize S----'s anyway. And, probably, after what many of them had encountered in their lives, they would likely have chosen to dismiss it as a relatively minor issue had they decided to stop.

The problem with S----'s lack of business wasn't the black lawn jockey statue. The problem was times had changed and the place hadn't. It just didn't swing, It's customers were few, old, drank little, ate and left early. It had zero late night action. And all the hot babes were hanging around the Left Guard where the Glen Cass band was playing rock and roll six nights a week, Packer players were gathering on their Monday nights off, and locals and out-of-towners alike were packing the place, eager to rub shoulders or bellies with either group, depending on whoever they were fortunate enough to join up with. So what Chuck was saying was total bullshit. Still, it gave him an opportunity to voice his displeasure. And it gave us a chance to have a little fun. We joined in, voicing our agreement. We knew we had Ross on the hook, and felt it wouldn't hurt to jerk him around a little.

"Well, Ross, nowadays blacks find those images of the old south offensive" we told him. "It's reminder of those days when they were the white man's slave."

Ross was troubled. "Hell, it's been there for years. It doesn't mean anything."

"It does now," we assured him, and Chuck added the clincher. " You know Coach Lombardi demands that all his players be treated equally. So if the black players find it offensive, the white players won't come here either."

Ross walked away from us, wiping down the bar, his brow furrowed. Evidently we had given him a lot to think about. We grinned among ourselves and went back to our dice game. We knew that S----'s was the kind of place where change, however slight, was regarded as highly dangerous. While we may have had the satisfaction of knowing we had struck a blow, however small, for racial dignity, we also knew probably little would come of it. It had, in reality, been little more than our pulling a practical joke, prompted by Ross's gullibility. However, we had vastly underestimated the human condition.

A couple of days later, as I approached the entrance, I stopped dead in my tracks, unable to comprehend what I was seeing. The lawn jockey ornament was still in its usual place but its black face and hands had been painted white. Not a flesh-colored pink, which would have been ghastly enough in its own right, but pure, picket fence, house-siding white. And, to add to the travesty, the black color under it had bled through so the total effect was a sickly greyish tone. Combined with the still grinning facial expression, it was so garishly loathsome it would have offended anyone based on aesthetics alone, let alone its initial racial slur. When I went inside Chuck was already there.

"Did you see it?" I asked in a hushed, incredulous tone. He nodded, his jaw clenched.

"Do you think it's a joke?"

Chuck's shrugged, his face twisted in disgust.

Ross came lopping over. "What'll you have?"

I searched his round, bland face carefully, looking for a clue that he had figured out we were jerking him around and had decided to respond in kind. But he was so blissfully unaware it was painful to see. Maybe someone else had done it? And Russ didn't know? But that notion was disposed of shortly.

I ordered my usual diet coke and after serving me Ross headed down the bar to wait on another customer. Chuck and I sat in silence as the others filed in, astonishment and disbelief on their faces. Their remarks were hushed, no one quite sure what to make of what our fooling around had wrought. Then Ray declared loudly to Ross, "Ross, your lawn boy out there needs another coat of white. He's looking kind of gray."

"You think so?" Ross asked earnestly, walking back to us. "Well, I was in kind of a hurry. You know," he whispered confidentially, "I wanted to take it away entirely but Dad didn't want to. Does it look ok?"

Well, not really, we told him. It looks like shit. He was crestfallen. "Well gee, I don't know what more I can do."

We went on with our usual afternoon routine although I noticed that Chuck was unusually quiet and withdrawn. When he took his turn at the dice, his rolls were lackluster, and he played without interest. Later that night, when we worked at the Left Guard, he had the early shift. After he got off he sat down at the bar for his after-work drink, looking serious. After while he called me over and we talked. Then he waited, drinking steadily, until bar time when he helped me close up. When we got to S----'s it was about two a.m. The interior was dark but several of the outdoor lights had been left on around the building for security. We hustled up the front steps, grabbed the lawn jockey from the entryway and put it on the car seat between us. As we hurtled down Highway 41 to our house, Chuck rolled down the window and pushed it out to drop on the concrete where it shattered into a hundred pieces.

"Great," I wise-cracked. "Not only can we get convicted of kidnapping but now it'll be murder as well."

Chuck didn't laugh. "Tough shit," he said tersely.

We drove home, had one more drink in silence, and went to bed. After that we started spending our afternoons at George's Steak House, a club a half a mile down the road from S----'s. A week or so later, another lawn jockey appeared in front of S----'s, in its original black-faced colors. The following year they closed their doors due to lack of business. By then Chuck was able to laugh a little when we'd recall the whole stupid affair.

13

Running With The White Bass

Another establishment I worked at was the Orihula Resort, located on the Wolf River. While places like The Horsefeather, The Left Guard and Nino's each had a lot of interesting and unique habituates and incidents, Orihula was definitely the champion, both in number, complexity and strangeness. It was one of those places which on first appearance seemed pretty ordinary, but my bartending career there was decidedly unusual. It only lasted about six months, but it yielded a large number of goofy happenings. Maybe it was just that time in my life.

Orihula Resort was located on the banks of the Wolf River, a few miles south on the town of Fremont. Why I got a job bartending there I'm not sure, since Fremont was located about 50 miles west of Appleton where I lived, a considerable drive back and forth. There were bars much closer to home where I could work. The best I can recall I was going through one of those times when I decided to find a new base of operations, to go to some area where nobody knew me, where I could re-invent my self and start over. This usually happened when I was going through a period of self-loathing due to my aimless, dissipated lifestyle.

Anyway, while the nomenclature "resort" nowadays tends to bring about images of luxurious vacations, the Orihula was a resort in a more basic definition. More like a glorified fishing camp, really. The main building sat close to the road on the inland side of a county highway, which ran closely parallel to the river. The main building was good-sized, having a basement, main floor and an upper floor. Inside a long bar ran along the river side of the main floor, with a string of big windows above the back bar with a view of the river. A large floor area held tables, game machines, a small stage off to one side, and a pool table. In the back part were living quarters and a kitchen. To one side off the bar was a dining room. The building, while clean, was old, built of wood, with a slightly shabby feel of hominess and comfort. In short, it was the kind of place where a blue-collar fishing guy would feel perfectly at ease.

Outside, the boat dock, bait house and a storage shed clung to a narrow strip of river bank across the highway. Adjoining the main building on the south was a two story motel building of a dozen rooms, with their doors opening to the outside. On the back of the property was a large, grassy area with sites for campers, RV's, and tents, with a shower/laundry building and a fish cleaning table at the center. All in all, a pretty typical lay-out, of which you could find a couple of hundred more like it throughout Wisconsin.

However, the Orihula held a significant difference. In the spring of the year, the Wolf River spawned (pun intended) an event know far and wide as the "white bass run."

White bass, a fish of about 3 to 4 pounds and 12 inches in length when grown, would hatch in the eddies and calmer backwaters along the shore in early summer. The minnows would then swim downstream and spend a leisurely year getting big and fat in the waters of Lake Winneconnie and Lake Winnebago, into which the Wolf flowed. The next spring the now adult fish would swim back upstream to spawn, an event lasting about two weeks. Ok, so imagine all those fish out in those two big lakes. Now funnel them together into the much smaller, narrower Wolf River. Now they are swimming upstream, battling the swift current, and like all of our species in springtime, they are focused on one thing--getting laid. As a result they are impatient, ornery, tired and voraciously hungry, snapping at anything and everything around them. Ta Da! It was said that during the white bass run, you could catch fish by poking a stick in the water and letting them bite onto it. That may be an exaggeration but not by much.

The limit during the run was something like 30 fish per day. So in a single afternoon you could go out and fish until your arms fell off. The white bass made for lousy eating unless pickled. But nobody caught them to eat. It was the catching them that made it fun for the fisherman. Or those who pretended to be.

And both types showed up, in numbers nearly as large as numbers of fish they were out to catch. On any given day during the run, it was not uncommon to see up to two dozen boats laden with fishermen within sight of the bar. How many more were scattered up and downstream could only be guessed at. And when they weren't on the river, they were at the Orihula. Now, some of my friends have accused me of occasionally being prone to exaggeration. But the following is God's truth. Some nights when I was tending bar during the run, as it got late in the evening, I would have to call the owner over and have him take some of the cash out of the till drawer as it was getting too full to close. Granted, the bills were ones, but still, it gives you some idea of the volume of business and the sheer number of customers packing the place.

The owner and operator of this operation was a lanky, dark-haired guy in his late forties named Earl D. Cigarette dangling from his lips, he would be on the premises constantly, rarely taking a day off. Helping him were his son Mike, son-in-law Kenny and his daughter Cathy. They were all about my age and we got along well. More importantly, having grown up on the river, they knew all about boats, fishing, local hot spots and such—in short, all the aspects of the resort business. I was city born and bred, and in our family the idea of a wilderness encounter was a picnic in the backyard. Hence, I found their help and advice invaluable since often I was (insert groan here) a fish out of water.

Earl was a soft-spoken former iron worker, with a hint of a drawl that suggested southern origins. He appeared to be easy-going. But, when necessary, he could exhibit the toughness and in-your-face, kick-your-ass attitude that was mandatory for anyone who once had worked in heavy construction's toughest and most dangerous trade. And he was never to particular to whom he'd address his comments, much to my bemusement.

I hadn't been working there very long when, one afternoon, a customer came in and sat down. I was busy setting up for the evening so Earl got up from his bar stool and walked behind the bar to wait on the customer.

"What'll you have?" Earl asked, cigarette dangling.

The customer, new to the place, took his time, surveying the bar and its contents.

Then, as is often the case when people aren't quite sure of what they'd like to drink,

he replied:

"Oh, I dunno."

Earl waited all of five seconds before he said, "Well, when you make up your fuckin' mind, let Bob know."

Then he walked back around the bar and returned to his seat. I was shocked. And much impressed. In my many years of tending bar I'd often been tempted to say something much like that to a vacillating customer. But of course, you never did. After all, the customer is always right, to be treated with courtesy. Right? Or not.

On another occasion a couple of women were staying with us. They did a little fishing but also spent time doing some day trips around the area, antiqueing and the like. One evening after dinner they came into the bar and spent a couple of hours there, drinking and socializing, joining in on the banter and goofing off that always goes on. Later they left and went to their room. About a half hour later, the phone rang. It was an angry guest, saying "somebody's outside banging on doors and yelling for Dollie. I'm getting up early to fish and this asshole won't stop." Evidently one of our male customers, his judgment clouded by alcohol, had misinterpreted the women' friendliness as his own personal invitation to a private party, and was trying to locate the room.

Earl kept a .357 Magnum in a holster on a shelf below the bar. He hung up the phone, grabbed it and headed out the door. He rounded the corner of the motel just as the man raised his fist, about to begin another barrage on a door.

"You touch that door again, and it'll be the last fuckin' thing you do," Earl hollered, raising the gun.

The man jerked around, turned ghostly white, and ran off into the darkness.

"He was running kind of funny," Earl chuckled later. "Like his pants were full of shit."

After I'd been there awhile I sometimes would screw around with the customers myself. Often some out-of-state visitor would be sitting at the bar and wonder aloud, "Orihula. That's an unusual name."

"It's an Indian word," I'd explain. "It means 'first high gathering ground after the rapids'." or some such bullshit. One time Earl overheard this exchange.

"Where did you hear that?" he demanded, coming over after the customer left.

"I looked it up," I lied.

He eyed me sceptically.

"Well. What does it mean?" I countered.

He shrugged. "Damned if I know. That was the name of the place when I bought it."

What was really weird was my explanation became accepted as truth. By the time I left in the fall I'd overheard quite a few times it being used by Mike and Kenny and other locals. Maybe I'd chosen the wrong career. I'd have done much better in a different one. Like politics.

Earl was also a shrewd business man, working any and all angles when it came to making a buck. He generally worried little about the legality of his methods. For instance, we of course sold fishing licenses. At the time, an in-state license sold for something like three dollars, an out-of-state six dollars. Earl would add on a one dollar "handling fee." This was illegal but he did it anyway. And in spite of the actual cost being printed right on the license, few people complained.

In addition to the licenses, we sold anything else you would need to fish. It would constantly amaze me how many men would show up with nothing but a rod and reel, to go fishing. This was partly due to Earl, a couple of times a week, being interviewed over the phone by a Chicago hook-and-bullet radio station. Regardless of conditions, he would always paint a glowing picture of the voracious white bass, walleye and other fish who were almost leaping into the fishing boats, like piscatorial kamikaze, so eager were they to be caught. So these guys would show up and we'd sell them the license, rent them the boat and the motor, sell them the gas, rent them the seat cushions—another illegal move, since the flotation devices were required by law— sell them the bait, sell them a six-pack and sandwiches and they'd finally be on their way. When they'd show up in the evening, complaining because they hadn't caught much, we would exhibit surprise, and work marketing psychology on them.

"Really? You got skunked? Well hell, just yesterday everybody out there caught their limit. Say, did you go south where that old dead tree sticks out in the river? You go there tomorrow, there's an eddy there where they like to hide in close to the bank. That's where you need to go...." And so on. So the next day out they'd go out again.

Earl was an equal opportunity violator when it came to

the law. He generally broke any of them that he felt interfered with his God-given right to make a profit, much like Milo Minderbender in Joseph Heller's *Catch 22*. Sometimes when I'd go downstairs to bring up beer and booze to restock the bar, he would be busily refilling the call liquor bottles such as Canadian Club, Jim Beam and the like—the good stuff we charged more for--with low-end booze of the same general flavor. "What the fuck," he'd say. "They don't know the difference. As long as they see it come out of the bottle with the CC label."

A unique accident of geography also enabled him to profit. The Orihula was located in the southwest corner of Winnebago County. This corner was cut off on a diagonal by the Wolf River, with the only bridge crossing the river in Fremont, about 8 miles to the north. Hence, any sheriff's patrol cars would have to cross the river into Fremont, turn left and proceed south before arriving at Orihula. The state mandatory bar closing time was 2 am. On a busy night during the white bass run, Earls' sole concession to this law would be to turn out the neon beer signs in the windows and dim the interior lights down to near darkness. Otherwise we kept pumping out drinks, the jukebox kept blaring and the cash kept rolling in, sometimes until the pink light of dawn was creeping through the windows. I found out later that on these nights Earl would give a six pack of beer to a friend and have him sit in his car at the bridge crossing in Fremont. If a Sheriff's car would appear he would go to a pay phone on the corner and warn Earl.

One of Earl's money-making ventures didn't fare so well. Someone upriver had a large pontoon boat for sale, the kind used to take people on river tours. Earl decided he would buy it, do a little remodeling, and turn it into a party boat. He would then rent it out, offering private cruises up and down the river, complete with booze, beer and food. "A real party boat," he explained.

While the remodeling work was being done, he approached Mike and Kenny about obtaining a commercial pilot's license from the Coast Guard, a necessity in order to take groups of any size out on the water. However, Mike and Kenny were less than enthusiastic. Disgruntled, Earl approached me. I was interested but seriously lacked any boating experience, let alone anything of this magnitude.

"Hell," Earl assured me. "There's nothing to it. It's like cruising up and down in your living room. I'll take you out a few times and show you the ropes."

It did sound pretty cool. I could see myself behind the wheel, suntanned, in shorts, my jaunty, gold-braided captain's hat at a rakish angle, surrounded by a bevy of horny, scantily clad bathing beauties, their faces agog with admiration at my manly nautical skills. But Mike brought me to my senses.

"Don't do it," he warned one night after taking me aside. "It's going to be a cluster-fuck. You'll be out there, stuck for hours with a boatload of drunks." Wisely I heeded his advice.

By now Earl was thoroughly miffed at our lackluster response. He adopted a screw-you-who-needs-you attitude and went and got the license himself. Within a week after the boat was ready he had booked his first event. A fraternity from Lawrence College in Appleton chartered the boat for a steak fry. They assured Earl everyone who would come on board was over twenty-one, so the charter cost included kegs of beer. "I'm making a bundle on my first trip," Earl chortled happily. "Those frat boys got money." So on a warm, sunny August Saturday, the frat boys came rolling up, jumping out of their cars, pumping fists in the air, yelling excitedly in anticipation. Toting back packs, clad in flip-flops, shorts and T-shirts, they ran up the gangplank, piling on the boat. Inside the bar myself and Kenny watched them scramble aboard, noting that it looked like many of them had gotten off to an early start with Bloody Marys. And a significant number looked to be under-age. But hey, it was none of our business.

Aboard the boat all was in readiness. The beer had been iced, charcoal grills fueled and tied to the deck rails, steaks and potato salad nestled in a neat row of coolers next to them. Earl had hired a couple of local women to do the cooking. Whether consciously or not, he had chosen a couple of older, hefty farm gals for this chore, about his only wise move of the whole event. With a hearty tooting of her whistle, cheering college boys lining the rail, the Orihula Queen proudly pulled away from the dock, her new white paint with blue trim glistening in the sun.

She returned at dusk, a sorry mess from stem to stern. While still a good ways away from the dock, we could make out Earl behind the wheel, his face grim and tight-lipped in anger. Those few frat boys now lining the rail were puking feebly in the water. As their desultory streams of vomit dwindled, they streaked the sides of the boat, already heavily stained with barf. A goodly number of them lay in heaps on the deck or sprawled on passenger benches, arms across their faces, too drunk to move. Kenny and Mike hurried down to the dock, helping with the lines as Earl brought the boat in. They ran out the gangplank and it had barely touched the dock when Earl stormed across, strode up the dock, crossed the road and charged into the bar. "Fuckin' college boys," he raged, angrily knocking over a bar stool as he crossed the room and disappeared into the back.

Outside the party-goers were staggering off the boat, their festive, gala mood gone. Several of them reached the road and promptly fell down, got up, fell down again, got up again, repeating this over and over, much to the hilarity of those of us watching from the bar. Over on the boat, Mike and Kenny were prodding the last few sorry-assed revelers to their feet and off the boat. Eventually they all made their way to their vehicles and slowly disappeared up the road. Back at the dock, Kenny had hooked up a hose and was washing down the deck and sides of the Queen while Mike unloaded the grills, coolers and trash. By dark they'd gotten her shipshape.

"Dad should have named it the Puke Bucket," Mike commented grimly as he sipped a beer at the bar afterward.

The next day Earl came out of seclusion and announced that henceforth the Queen would be chartered only for family events and the like. He kept to his word and in time he did have quite a few charters, But none of them like her maiden voyage.

Often on week-end nights in the summer we featured live music. Some nights it would be a polka band, others a country music trio. Still another act was a singer named Hap Hogan. Hap worked alone, singing country tunes and old time favorites while playing rhythm guitar. One busy night one of a group of fishermen who were at the place for the white bass run approached the stage and chatted with Hap. After a few minutes, Hap brought the guy up on stage and gave him his guitar.

"Ladies and gentlemen," Hap announced over the PA, "Here's special treat for all of us. Let's give a big hand and and a nice listen to one of country music's biggest stars, T. Texas Tyler!"

Now I was somewhat familiar with country music but sorry, I'd never heard of this guy. And I don't know how many others in the bar had, either. But you didn't have to hear more than the first couple of lines of his opening number and you could tell this guy was really good. He looked worn, and his face held the kind of pale fatigue that indicated ill health, likely the result of a hard living lifestyle . With a days' growth of whiskers on his leathery face, dressed in his wrinkled fishing clothes topped by a cowboy hat, he was an unlikely looking country music star. But he had a stage presence and a voice that magically made the seedy place and rowdy crowd transform itself into a concert stage with a top country band and himself in a sequined outfit glistening in the bright lights as he sang of heartbreak, good whiskey and bad women.

He finished his first number and the place went nuts. He did a half a dozen more before he stepped down, pleading fatigue after a long day on the river. He rejoined his buddies at the bar and for the rest of the night the other customers bought them round after round of drinks.

I learned later that this man indeed had been a bona fide country star. Born David Luke Myrick in Mena ,Arkansas, T. Texas Tyler had a very successful career from 1946 to 1954, playing on the Grand Old Opry, the Louisiana Hayride and, ultimately, Carnegie Hall. In 1948, he wrote and recorded a spoken-word hit single entitled "The Deck of Cards." It was his biggest hit, and told the story of a World War Two soldier who explains how a deck of playing cards serves as his Bible, almanac and prayer book. He followed it up with another smash entitled "Dad Gave My Dog Away." (Yeah, I know, they don't write them like that anymore.) He died in 1972, at the age of 55.

A popular fishing boat frequently seen up and down the river was the Ouachita. It was an aluminum, flat-bottomed fishing boat, painted olive drab, powered by an outboard motor. They were roomy, with the fourteen and sixteen footers able to easily handle two or three fishermen and their gear. With their flat bottoms, the boats were ideal for moving into the shallower waters where the fish would be lurking. Also, these flat bottoms made the boats stable, a plus when a fisherman needed to get up and move about. However, they were not unsinkable, a fact I found out one day while bartending.

It was a nice, sunny, spring afternoon and the river was liberally sprinkled with boats of fishermen. Through the windows above the back bar we could see several, and the regulars sitting at the bar sipping their beers would keep an eye on the anglers as they fished, commenting when one of them would haul in a nice sized bass or wall-eye. One boat directly across from the bar held three fishermen, one in the bow, one in the middle and one near the stern. While the boats around them were hauling in fish, for some reason they weren't having much luck. After about 45 minutes, they reeled in the lines, and got ready to move to a different location.

The anchor rope on this particular craft was tied at the stern, next to the outboard motor. The man seated in the back began to pull it in but the anchor was snagged and wouldn't budge. He tugged harder but nothing happened. The man in the middle got up and stepped to the back, where he also began to help pull. The rear of the boat dipped ominously further into the water from the additional weight. By now the plight of the three had caught the interest of everyone at the bar.

"You know," one of the locals said sagely, "if that guy in front moves back there to help, that boat's going in the drink."

As if we were on a Hollywood movie set and our local was the director who has just given the cue, the guy in front got up and stepped back to help his buddies. And, sure enough, just when he reached them, the boat reared up, and in a flash slipped neatly stern-end first into the water. A moment later three heads, one still with a hat on, bobbed gently in the water, amid an array boat cushions, minnow bucket, tackle boxes and other flotsam. But the boat was gone.

Those of us who'd witnessed this bit of slapstick comedy broke into peals of laughter. You couldn't help it. The Three Stooges couldn't have done it any better. Since they were wearing life vests, the three guys were in no immediate danger. And the other boats around them began to quickly make their way over to lend assistance. We were still laughing when some minutes later the unfortunate trio was deposited on shore, along with as much of their gear that could be salvaged. As they made their to the parking lot, leaving a trail of wet footprints and rivulet of dripping water, a local wag dubbed them 'the three Houdinis, because they made a boat disappear.'

Several days later they were back. The DNR, when hearing of the accident, tracked them down and told them they had to get the boat out of the river. So they hired a local river rat with the necessary equipment and skill to retrieve the boat. It took most of the afternoon to perform the operation and, while it was interesting to watch, it wasn't nearly as funny as when it happened.

On another occasion I nearly ended up in the water myself, under circumstances which were no laughing matter. At my time working at Orihula, I was a total landlubber. I'd maybe been in a boat a half a dozen times in my life, when someone would invite me along on a pleasure jaunt. The few times I'd ever fished it had been with my feet planted on shore, using a cane pole with worms for bait.

One evening after I got off of work, Mike, Kenny and a group of their friends decided to go to Winniconnie, to Mulligan's Bar. Winnieconnie was a village on the western shore of a lake with the same name, and Mulligan's was right at the shore. The lake was fed by the Wolf River, so the fastest and most direct route was by boat, down the river and across the lake. It was after dark when we all piled into Mike's 16 foot Ouachita and made the trek. As we motored on our way, I noticed that we seemed to be really low in the water. But hey, there were seven of us in the boat. And everyone of my companions had grown up along the river, and were veteran river rats. So if no one else seemed very concerned, why should I be?

We had a good time at Mulligan's. It a dark, mildly dingy saloon with a lot of fishing gear hanging all over to give it ambiance. Its one really unique attraction was a concrete tank over in one corner which held a live alligator.

Sadly, the animal seemed in pretty bad condition, floating listlessly in the confines of its smelly water. I'm sure its condition wasn't helped much by the fact that virtually everyone who came there would sooner or later toss junk food or pour beer into its tank, ignoring a sign that forbade such activity. A few foolish souls, fortified by liquor, would stick their hand in the water, again despite a warning sign. If the critter hadn't been in such bad shape, it probably would have snapped off a few fingers, just out of frustration.

We'd been hanging around Mulligan's for quite a while, getting boisterously drunk, having fun. I began to work my charms on one of the young ladies, a pert little blonde who was a friend of Mike's wife. Then the rumble of thunder and flash of lightning outdoors began to get our attention.

"Shit," Kenny remarked, "we're gonna get a wet ass on the ride home."

"Maybe we should wait until ii blows over," someone suggested, an idea that made a great deal of sense to everyone. So we bellied up to the bar and continued to drink. By now you can probably predict what happened. It didn't blow over. If anything, the storm continued to get worse, fat raindrops hammering down, the wind picking up, while we continued to ignore it, snug and warm inside the bar. And then our clever plan was thwarted by the tyranny of the state liquor code.

"Drink 'em up," Mulligan hollered. "It's bar time. I

don;t care where you go but you can't stay here."

Minutes later we were huddled outside under the bar's overhang, glumly confronting our predicament. Around us the rain pounded down, the wind battered the building. In the windows behind us the beer signs snapped off and we could hear Mulligan firmly slam the front door, locking it, leaving us to our fate.

Time slipped by. We lit cigarettes and muttered curses, our bar room euphoria banished by life's cruel ironies. Finally the storm began to ease somewhat. "Well, hell," someone said. "It won't get any better. Let's make a run for it."

So we did.

While the rain had let up, not so the wind. The lake was covered with white caps, hampering our progress. And sloshing water into the boat. We hadn't gone more than 50 feet from the dock when Kenny and another guy picked up a couple of plastic milk jugs with half the tops cut off and began to bail methodically. I looked around worriedly. But no one else seemed at all bothered. The girls were amorphous shapes seated in the darkness after pulling their jackets over their heads for protection. Mike sat stoically at the thwart, hand on the outboard's handle, steering us across the lake towards the river. As the shore line receded in the darkness, I continued to feel a twinge of alarm. There were a few life jackets lying in the bottom of the boat but not nearly enough for everyone. And besides, wasn't it women and children first? It would probably be in really poor taste if I'd be seen slugging the very woman I'd been trying to fondle in the bar, while I wrested the life jacket from her hands as the boat sank. I felt the water slosh around me ankles. Was it getting deeper? It sure felt like it. And the top of the boat seemed barely above the water. An occasional flash of lightning showed a shoreline barely visible in the rainy distance. Too far to swim. Oh Christ. I'm going to die. I closed my eyes and prayed in a whimpering silence to God to save my worthless ass.

After an eternity I felt the wind let up. I opened my eyes and squinted into the darkness. Mike was still at the helm, the guys were still bailing, the laden boat still putting along barely above the water. All was as before, with no one the least bit worried. Except me. But now I could see we had entered the river, the shorelines much closer on either side. I felt a glimmer of hope. If we sank now, maybe I could make it to shore.

After several more lifetimes I saw the Orihula dock lights in the distance. We gradually drew closer, than we were alongside. Thank you God. As we scrambled onto the dock, Kenny turned to Mike and said:

":Shit, I didn't think we were going to make it."

"Me either," Mike replied.

I searched their faces in the yellow light, to see if they were kidding each other. They were drop-dead serious. I felt a heart attack coming on. "You pricks," I muttered.

They eyed me curiously as I turned and walked up the dock, across the road, and got into my car. All the way to Appleton I had the heater on full blast but was still shaking with cold when I got home. That had to be the reason. It couldn't have been fear.

14

Changing Times

At its heyday in the 1960s, the Left Guard Steak House chain did a booming business. By the early 1970s, it had expanded to eleven locations in several states, grossing in the millions of dollars in sales. Initially Max and Fuzzy spent most of their time at the Appleton flagship location but as the business expanded, they often would depart to check on operations and be seen at other locations. But in time business began to slow.

After Vince Lombardi left the organization, The Packers went into a lengthy period of dismal losing seasons. The glory of the championship years faded. Where at one time fans would be willing to kill to get a ticket to a sold-out Packer game, now tickets were readily available, often given away on Sundays by those who chose not to attend the games. New players filled the roster and younger fans found new favorites among them. Gradually the heroes of the Lombardi era faded from view as they took on new lives in other places. Willie Davis invested in a successful beer dealership in the Los Angeles area. Paul Hornung was an early owner in KFC. Bart Starr had an interest in an auto dealership in his native Alabama, but returned to the Packers as head coach during the late 1970's. Forrest Gregg continued in football as a head coach of college and NFL teams, including a stint with the Green Bay Packers. Ken Bowman became a lawyer. Doug Hart secured a partnership in a snowmobile manufacturing company. Jerry Kramer authored several books, including his classic auto-biography, *Instant Replay*. My life changed as well, as I pursued other full time occupations while continuing to bar tend at the Left Guard part-time.

Along with the gradual ebbing of Packer fame, social habits changed. The health profession began to emphasize the dangers of some of the prime components of the very things that made the Left Guard Steak Houses so popular. Cigarette smoking, alcohol consumption, eating charcoal cooked meats, all were declared unhealthy. In addition, law enforcement and state legislators, due to the alarming increase in alcohol-related traffic deaths and other abuses, began to pass laws with much stricter penalties for those who offended.

In addition, the financing required for the rapid expansion of the chain had been substantial. As interest rates began to rise drastically during the 70s, it impacted negatively on the entire operation.

As a life-long Packer fan, along with many others, I found it very difficult to see the Packer team struggle through those years of decline. It was also sad and disheartening for me to see Max, and especially Fuzzy, struggle with the decline of their Left Guard restaurants.

In the Appleton location, the place where I'd had so many good times, it was difficult to watch the drifting apart of all those great people I'd worked with, as well as all the wonderful, crazy regulars. All of those folks, both famous and not, that I'd met, partied with, and grew so fond of.

Gradually, one by one, the Left Guards began to close. In time Max sold his interest in the business to Fuzzy and other investors and went on to develop the highly successful Chi Chi's Mexican restaurant chain. He also became an extremely popular color commentator for radio broadcasts of the Packer games. From 1979 to 1998, broadcasting alongside Jim Irwin, his droll humor and sometimes cutting analysis of the on-the-field action entertained Packer fans everywhere. It was not unusual during that time to walk into a bar or home and find, that while the Packer game was on the TV set, the audio was turned off, while the play by play boomed from the radio courtesy of Jim and Max. In time he set aside his boisterous life style and married, settling in the Twin Cities with his wife Denise and raising four sons. William Max McGee died in a fall in from his house roof in 2007.

Eventually, faced with bankruptcy, Fuzzy sold his remaining interest in the Left Guard chain to a few local business people. By this time only the Appleton Left Guard and one in Madison were operating. He opened up Fuzzy's Steak House in Menasha and later a bar called Shenanigan's in Green Bay. There was virtually nothing left of the financial gains he had accrued in prior years. He was forced to sell his cars, house, cottage and business interests. But he and Sue dug in and began again, working together as a team to run Shenanigans. As they began to get ahead, another, more frightening obstacle arose. In 1980 Fuzzy was diagnosed with throat cancer. After several operations and with a lot of hard work, he manged to beat the odds and survive, eventually regaining his speaking ability. Through these downturns of his life, Sue remained his greatest inspiration, supporting him both emotionally and financially. Now 79 years of age, he owns and operates Fuzzy's Bar in Green Bay. In spite of all the ups and downs in his many-faceted career as Packer player, restaurant owner and businessman, he is still the great, open-hearted, gregarious man he's always been. His grown children have families of their own and he's a proud father, grandfather and still married to Sue, his high school sweetheart. Looking back on those years of working for him and Max, I consider myself fortunate that my path crossed with both of theirs.

One day one of their number would write a book about all this, but none of them would believe it, because none of them would remember it that way.

James Jones, <u>The Thin Red Line</u>

The End

APPENDEX

Max McGee   No. 85 Wide Receiver
Date of birth: July 16, 1932
Place of birth: Overton, Texas
Date of death: Oct 20, 2007
Place of death: Deephaven, Minnesota

Career
College football:
Tulane
Pro Football:
Green Bay Packers 1954, 1957-1967
Debuted in 1954. Last played in 1967

Highlights:
Green Bay Packers Hall of Fame
First team Pro Bowl Selection 1961
Scored the first touchdown in Super Bowl
history, 1966

NFL Statistics:
Receptions 345
Receiving Yards   6,346
Touchdowns   50

Fred "Fuzzy" Thurston   No. 63 Left Guard

Date of birth: Dec 29, 1933

Place of birth: Altoona, Wisconsin

Career

College football:

Valparaiso

Pro Football:

NFL Draft: 1956, Round 5, pick 54

Debuted in 1958. Last played in 1967

Baltimore Colts 1958

Green Bay Packers 1959-1967

Highlights:

Green Bay Packers Hall of Fame

First Team AP All-Pro 1961

Second Team AP All-Pro 1962

Player on Six NFL Champion Teams 1958,   1961, 1965-1967

NFL Statistics:

116 Games

Additional Reading

Instant Replay, by Jerry Kramer and Dick Schaap, Doubleday Publishing, 1968, 2006

What a Wonderful World, by Fuzzy and Sue Thurston with Bill Wenzel, copyright 2006